SUB-
MISSIVE

candid interviews
with 20 lifestyle
submissives

COMPILED & EDITED BY ROY TURNER

MAGNOLIA BOOKS

Contents

About the writer

Born in London in 1952, Roy Turner graduated from Middlesex University and Saint Martins School of Art. He studied sociology and anthropology and wrote several historical biographies based on his extensive travels around the world.

Roy Turner was best known as the founder and editor of the fetish magazine Domina. Earlier career re-incarnations included teaching, acting, painting and decorating, carpentry, window dressing and window cleaning. He also worked briefly in a Wild West Rodeo in Arizona and had a shot at bullfighting in Spain.

Sadly, Roy died in 2007 after a long battle with cancer, but his diligent research and unique insights into the sadomasochistic world live on. A sister volume 'Dominatrix' featuring interviews with 20 female dominants, also compiled and edited by Roy Turner, is also published for the first time by Magnolia Books.

Introduction

'Submissive', explores the largely hidden world of the submissive and masochistic female. The 20 selected interviews here were conducted over a 10-year period, by the BDSM magazine publisher and writer, Roy Turner and offer a full, frank and totally unique insight into the real world of the lifestyle submissive.

It certainly isn't some E L James 'Fifty Shades of Grey' or Nancy Friday 'My Secret Garden', etc fantasy-fest, what it does show is that those stereotypes—if they exist at all, are just not at all representative of the experiences related here. Like her male counterpart, the submissive female comes in all types; she can quite often be a highly successful career woman in 'real' life that simply craves the occasional release from responsibility that comes through role-play, or a women who throws herself headlong into the lifestyle 100%. There was also a tendency to separate 'Husbands/Lovers' from 'Masters' and carry on a double-life either with or without their partner's knowledge or consent. But there is also a much darker side too that is not found so much in the male submissive; a truly dangerous area that some women willingly step into.

These women certainly 'walk the talk'; whether it is extreme role-play, slave training, pony-girl, enforced servitude and prostitution, abduction or even kidnapping. Consequently, some of the experiences related here could be considered extremely shocking and genuinely disturbing. It's definitely not one for the faint-hearted!

For many interviewees, the need for domination had its roots, not surprisingly, in childhood. An authoritarian, even brutal, father—who went way beyond the occasional spanking, etc, started a trend, which they sought to recreate in future relationships. But other subjects found themselves instinctively drawn to it for reasons less explicable, certainly not out of diminished self-esteem or anything that obvious. In many of the stories told, the division between controlled and controller becomes blurred, in other words, the so-called submissive is actually directing the scenario. By far the most popular and powerful scenario for most women was the idea of being used by two or more men, total humiliation and degradation often being the key driver.

A submissive is rarely passive, but invariably an active participant in the action, often directing the scenario 'from below' and letting the dominant man or woman know exactly what she wants. As one slave-girl put it: "A woman will follow where she wants to be led".

Publisher's Note: This book contains explicit sexual content, graphic language, and situations that some readers may find objectionable. It is intended for an adult audience.

Chapter 1: Janesca

Age: 36, Location: Lincolnshire, United Kingdom

Though I am now a confirmed sexual submissive, nothing in my happy Dutch childhood, or very normal early sexual experimenting, even remotely hinted at the perverse pleasure I now take in my adoptive role. That knowledge was revealed to me in 1985 when I first came to live in Britain at the age of twenty one to do a years post graduate work. The knowledge so altered my life that I have lived, and loved, here ever since.

I appreciate that you're probably more interested in my sexual history, but that may be better understood if you know something of me as a whole person. You see, in my wider life there is absolutely nothing whatsoever submissive about me. I have always been a competitive sports person and a high academic achiever. My work environment is one of small, integrated scientific teams. My job, at present, is research work for a large international company. Incidentally, my HR manager commented that I hadn't operated at my best until I was appointed as a Team Leader. I say this not to boast, but to make people understand that in my normal life I am very assertive. Close friends, and non-sexual men friends in particular, have even criticised me in the past for being socially aggressive. Incidentally, this is something I refute as simply a cultural difference. It has nothing to do with my nature. Dutch women do not defer to males in the subtle ways most English women still seem to. All in all, nobody knowing me socially or professionally would recognise the persona

I adapt to in a sexual environment. That persona is specific and limited to that particular sphere of activity.

A point I want people to understand is that my sexual behaviour is self chosen because this is what excites me. It is not because I am incapable of acting otherwise, or because of some long concealed psychological defect resulting from a childhood trauma. I like what I do, or rather, what I let others do. The thrill for me is the abnegation of self. I particularly like group sex where I become an object used without any consideration for my gratification. The first New Man who asks me what I want from a sexual experience would be very surprised and probably very hurt! I mean that I'm a very good Kick Boxer! I want to be told what to do, commanded, required to satisfy a man's needs. I like sex to be strong and raw and very potent. No pretence of gentle love. I don't want to be asked, because that involves me in taking or sharing responsibility for what happens to me. I want the selfish freedom of total obedience, of commands that give no option of choice and, as a logical extension of that, absolutely no guilt.

I want the privilege of saying to myself after a truly disgusting night, "Well, I was only obeying orders". That way one can indulge in the most debasing activity and feel totally humiliated, but wipe the slate clean of remorse afterwards with that as an excuse and motivation.

Okay, we'll start with me after six months in, well, let's just say somewhere in England. I had, by this time, got used to being chased by men in that curious amalgam of sexual crudity and courteous good humour that one only finds in this country. I attract that kind of attention a lot. I know I am exotically good looking. I am dark skinned with large brown eyes and long black hair. I am fine boned and rather small and petite. There were quite a few Indonesian imports into my family tree. The typical youthful Englishman's propensity to treat me as some exotic but, essentially, dim-witted doll was seriously counter productive and I resisted all attempts at seduction with little effort.

My studies threw me into contact with Vernon, a man in his

early forties. Here was a quintessential Englishman, I thought. A tall, lean, supercilious iceberg on the outside, with a volcano hidden within. He was always polite and thoroughly correct in a work environment, but forever holding an invisible shield between himself and any real involvement. In a rare social moment I allowed him to know I might like a little less formality in our contacts. As a consequence, he kindly threw a small party for me on my birthday. I repaid him by getting slightly drunk. He had never, by word, look or gesture, indicated any interest in me as a woman. A sexual woman, I mean. This intrigued me. I wondered if he was queer. He bought a stone bottle of 'Zuidam' Jonge Genever—a particularly refined Dutch gin, especially for my benefit. The beauty of those bottles is no one notices how much one consumes. I consumed a lot and became inquisitive. I inquired why he had never made a pass at me. Didn't he fancy me?

We were sat on the stairs. He was one lower than me. Our heads were level. He admitted that, of course, he fancied me. I asked why he had never tried his luck? I can still remember his soft laugh when he explained the reason. He admitted he had, as he put it, strange tastes that would revolt me. The kind of games he played would not only revolt me, but hurt and frighten me, too. He told me that, in his games, he liked laughter at the beginning, tears in the middle and loud cries at the end. Those cries may be of satisfaction or of pain. With the kind of women he liked there, apparently, isn't that much difference.

To this day I don't know why I pressed the point. I'd never had any great interest in him as a man. For a start, he was too old for me. And I certainly had never imagined any involvement in the kind of activity he hinted at. Sadomasochistic clubs are an accepted part of normal sexuality in Holland. I can't even pretend his words unleashed any secret desire. It was just what's often been described as my bloody mindedness that made me respond with a calculated challenge. "I thought you were supposed to be a scientist? You shouldn't theorise without evidence. Why don't you conduct an experiment?"

In answer, he leaned over, I thought to kiss me. I lifted my face. He asked, in a whisper, if I really wanted to? I nodded. He put his mouth to mine. His hand came up and cupped my breast. I grew a little breathless and then suddenly pain lanced through me as he bit my lip hard. I went to draw away, but he held me. His teeth slackened, and then his fingers found the nipple through the thin material of my dress. He laughed into my mouth as he felt it harden and then he began to squeeze with vice like fingers. Every girl has done that to herself, sometimes let a girlfriend do it. But this was more agonising than anything I'd experienced before. He whispered again in my ear, telling me all I had to do was ask him to stop. However, in my mind the challenge had been set, the gauntlet thrown down, and I would not ask. Instead, I let him continue till, at last, his own aching fingers gave way. Only then did I cry as the blood rushed back into the constricted knot of flesh. But I still watched him steadily through my tears.

Have you ever noticed how ice cool eyes can suddenly become hot anticipating orbs? He lifted his glass to me and jokingly punned that perhaps I was looking for Dutch Courage in my drink. I giggled and told him that it was rather Dutch Fear, in my case. None the less, I agreed to carry on the experiment and meet him in private that next afternoon.

Before I go on to describe what resulted from that gin lubricated talk, let me just add this. Many people, like me, will have had a conventional religious upbringing. This results in adding to sins attraction, but leaves one rather prone to guilt. Some of my internal disquiet was reduced a few days later by hearing a cleric mouthing in the wake of a tragic murder and rape. He was counselling calm to the bereaved relatives, but I felt he could just as easily have been talking about me and my situation.

He was asking why such things happen? Why a powerful being submits to such awfulness. Why not resist it? Stop it? I will tell you! Because nothing is so powerful as submission! How better to prove strength than by refusing to exert it? Overcome power by bowing to it. How better to exert ultimate superiority than by controlling oneself, not others? A willing submission denies the tyrant his triumph. Recall the story of the turned cheek. Who was the stronger? The striker or the struck?

I felt I had a spiritual sanction for an action I felt oddly compelled to see through. I approached that first meeting with trepidation, rather than excitement. No more than an intellectual curiosity and a childish sense of daring. Imagine my confusion to find not one man there, but two! Vernon sensed my nervousness and laughed, assuring me that, while he was peculiar, he was wasn't queer! His friend, Raymond, was someone, apparently, who shared his interests. And he meant, quite literally, shared! He informed me that what I was prepared to offer him, I should offer Raymond as well.

In my innocence I was relieved. My initial response had been that a third party might provide some restraint. It did, but not in the way I had thought. The restraint would be applied to me, but I'll come to that in due course. I also felt, I must admit, the first stirrings of excitement. Raymond was much closer to my own age. Less than thirty, very handsome, and with an engaging smile. I liked that smile. He smiled a lot that afternoon, especially when I cried. Strangely, I was made to feel that everything that was done to me was somehow justified as long as he smiled.

Vernon was very clever, and very patient. To this day I don't know if he magically imposed a new persona upon me or merely revealed one that already existed deep within me. What I do know is that I experienced, for the first time, the phenomenon of what I call 'my other self'. It was as though another being took over my body. The 'I' retreated into a quiet corner and became an observer, not a participant. An observer making rational comments that this 'other self'' had no wish to hear and, for the most part, ignored.

Initially, I was required to make the running. On the coffee table there were books and magazines dealing with flagellation. Vernon suggested I look at some and discuss them. The condition was that with each new volume I picked up I would be required to remove one piece of clothing. There was an odd, humiliating excitement gradually becoming naked in front of two fully dressed men.

As concerned talking about the activities described in the magazines, I knew little and what I found was, I admit, mildly shocking.
Looking back on that afternoon, I came to appreciate how fortunate
I was to have such considerate mentors in the disciplinary arts. A
more brutal introduction would not have inflamed me in the way it
did. In fact, not until I had actually begged them to do anything, did
either man attempt to really hurt me or physically control me. It all
began with the mind games.

They could see what disturbed me in the magazines I flipped
through and they made me talk about them. They asked me to imagine myself in the position described or pictured. They asked how
I thought the girl felt. They required me to describe how I thought
I would respond in her place. As I say, they were clever. Whenever
that line of questioning got too much for me, I would toss that volume aside and select another, sacrificing an item of clothing in the
process in order to avoid disturbing questions, so they won either
way! They also made it clear that I was free to leave at any point. In
fact, their cleverest ploy was to suggest several times that I do just
that. Naturally, this only made me more determined to stay!

To cut a long story short, discussions soon turned to demon-
strations. I was required to request each man in turn to spank me. I
found it was not unduly painful, but neither did it physically excite
me. In fact, I noticed another peculiarity about myself. In these kind
of situations I seem to develop an incredibly high pain threshold.
No, sorry, that's not quite accurate. I feel the pain, of course. I weep
and cry out at it, but I don't somehow have the limits I would have
in normal life. I can, and will, endure almost anything I am commanded to. What that first spanking did for me was to create an
intense feeling of childish humiliation that ended up bringing me
close to orgasm. My responses were more emotional than physical.
I found myself seeking their approval and wanting to please. They
interspersed the spanking by making me stand or kneel or crouch
in various provocative and blatant poses, which I also found very
exciting. They would then make me masturbate and lick my fingers
one by one. Made me put my wet fingers up my arse, then lick them

again. I found myself actually begging them to resume the spanking. Only when I pleaded 'nicely' enough, did they do it.

In fact, it was me who suggested to them that my introduction wouldn't be complete without experiencing the strap and the cane. However, Raymond felt that this was too advanced a step, considering my inexperience. He felt that I would not have the self control required to submit and would need to restrained. Of course, this was another clever trick on his part. Naturally, as soon he said that, I couldn't be denied, and he knew it! I found myself dissolving at the very thought of being helpless and at their mercy. The more they warned me that I wouldn't be shown any mercy, the more idiotically I insisted they should carry on. It was a very bizarre scenario! There was me pleading with them to be tied up and thrashed, while they both warned me in graphic detail of what they intended doing to me!

In actual fact, in comparison with later developments, they were fairly restrained with me. I had to choose who was to apply the strap and who was to wield the cane. I selected Vernon to strap me as my mental picture of Raymond with a cane in his hand had a 'phallic' symbolism all too perfectly understandable to that quaking, hidden rational self.

I wept a great deal. Both men used me sexually; my mouth, my arse, my hands, but never my vagina. They filled my sex organ with their fingers and tongues and various toys. A cucumber even played a part. But they never used their cocks, which further degraded me. Although I was deeply stirred, I didn't climax at all during the whole event.

Raymond drove me home that night, after about four or five hours of play, because by then I was in no state to make my own way. I invited him in for a 'coffee', leaving him in no doubt as to my ulterior motive. He ended up staying the night. He was very gentle, yet very ardent. The sex then was the best I've ever had. In fact, I was the animal, not him. I was insatiable and very noisy. I wanted the world to know how good it was. It's been like that with me ever since. I find that I rarely peak while actually playing games, but am primed for a long orgy immediately afterwards.

After that first session, it was left to me to suggest further meetings. They became quite regular, one or two a week sometimes. I was constantly bruised. They would invite one or two other men along, as well as the occasional submissive girl to join me for punishment. Some three months later, they took me to my first 'punishment party'. There were about twenty men there, as well as two other girls. It was harsh and unremitting, with the men spurring each other on and a new one taking over as soon as one flagged. I found myself being subjected to more pain than I would have imagined it possible to bear. There was also a strange feeling of sisterhood amongst us fellow female sufferers. Without any verbal agreement, we each knew when a girl had momentarily reached her limit and initiated strategies to divert attention. Sometimes we would actually claim her place at the whipping post out of 'jealousy'.

Strangely enough, there wasn't an awful lot of sex going on at these events, except for a lot of cock sucking, which I found degrading, but in an oddly delightful way. The ultimate humiliation was in being raffled, along with the other two girls, to see which man would have us as his bed mate for the rest of the night. I both resented and gloried in that. As it turned out, the man who won me was a useless lover and no help to me in my urgent need. I was still boiling when Raymond came to collect me in the morning. I made him pull off the road at the first opportunity in order to give me the good screwing I so desperately needed by this time. We fucked for an hour in some muddy field before I had calmed down enough to resume the journey home. Once at my place, we went straight to bed and stayed there for the next thirty six hours!

At the end of my years study there was no question of me going home to Holland. I found work in England and continued to see Raymond, but rather less of Vernon. It was an odd relationship, but very satisfying, in it's own way. We never socialised in the ordinary sense. I found my own circle of friends for my normal social life. As he put it, my time with him was strictly cock and cane! Amongst my fellow Submissives I developed a taste for lesbian love. Naturally, outside of the disciplinary circle I became chaste. This was done both out of choice and necessity. After all, how would I ever explain to a 'straight' lover all my bruises and scars? In any case, sex without the preliminary stimulus of degradation and pain had lost its saviour. I had proved that to myself when I once persuaded Raymond to come away with me on a weekend trip. Without the element of discipline it proved highly unsatisfactory for both of us. We drove home early on the Sunday morning and never tried that silly experiment again!

As I understand it, I'm not required to give a 'blow by blow' account of my induction into the masochistic world. For this I'm grateful. Any woman who has been so regularly whipped will tell you that the experience becomes a blur. Only the observer differentiates the time, the tool used and the savagery or artistry of the user. For the receiver, there are only two points of reference. Those are the flood and ebb of the pain and the voice of the Master. It may encourage or denigrate, insult or praise, but one listens to that voice with greater attention than to the whine of the descending whip.

What outsiders fail to appreciate is that the submission game, like sex itself, although apparently a bodily function, is in reality a shadow play in the mind. What happens on the skin only serves to supplement what goes on in the psyche. I have discovered that to submit is the greatest liberation of all. Restrained and 'helpless' under the whip, I have a freedom few women ever know. A conventional woman, no matter how excited, either through self interest, love or just courtesy, still considers her lover's feelings. Massage his ego, compliment his technique, admire his physique, wilt under his stamina, praise his virility. All this and yet still maintain an image in his eye that will grace his table.

As a submissive, I have no such obligation. I can be utterly, selfishly absorbed by my own feelings to the exclusion of all else. All I have to do is obey my Master's command and accept whatever he chooses to do to me. Paradoxically, as a masochist, I have no obligation to make an effort to please him. In fact, he is, quite literally, pleasing himself, and me, using my body as the vehicle. For my part, I can simply focus my energies on returning to that pain filled 'sweatiness' that is our common genesis. I can sweat and fart, scream and weep at that most fundamental level that civilisation strives so hard to deny us. There is an incredible primitive pleasure in screaming that has nothing to do with the degree of hurt. It is simply a release of, and from, everything.

For example, I have frequently been made to piss myself, either as a reactive, that is, relinquishing of control due to excessive pain, sometimes even of pleasure, or simply from being kept in restraints for a longer period than my bladder can sustain. Once I even shit myself and was cruelly whipped for it. I carry the scars to this day. But where a 'normal' woman might carry long memories of shame at such ill treatment, my shame is immediate and profoundly satisfying. It's also forgotten the moment my shackles are removed. Nothing that happens to me under duress (however secretly I permit or desire it) is really my responsibility. Basically, from my point of view, he did it and he made me do it! At the price of a little temporary pain, I'm freed of any limit to my most indulgent and primitive desires.

We females are closer to our genetic inceptions than men, both in body and in mind. The process of our monthly bleeding reminds us both of our designated function and our relationship to the animal kingdom. Men try to distance themselves from this. Only men could create a religion that denies sex its pivotal role and asks its priests to remain virginal. The ancient female religions celebrated nature by having its priestess's play the whore and give themselves to worshippers on the temple steps, thus celebrating the gift of sex in congress as close to the altar as they could get. My whippings strip the 'sophistication's' from me. I can't pretend, I can't pose, I can only be... me!

Anyway, back to my story. I was promoted at work, which meant I had to move home. I was overjoyed professionally, but desperately worried about how it would affect my 'secret life'. Raymond simply shrugged his indifference and, a week later, informed me that he had 'transferred' me to a new master in Lincolnshire who would allow him visiting rights. I don't know how to explain the strange gratification I got from the knowledge that I had been disposed of like a slave at an auction!

During the flurry of moving and the resultant hiatus, I had a brief, mad interlude of a marriage to a kind, but straight, man that lasted less than six months. We parted without bitterness. It was a mistake. I still use his name though, which is why I can reveal my maiden name. Anyway, I soon returned to my old ways of sexual servitude as Raymond had decreed. I am still with that master; actually, a duo of masters! Two brothers. Within the restricted confines of rural Lincolnshire I meet both of them quite often, both professionally and socially. By convention, our exchanges have to be limited as they are both married. As I'm still in my thirties and considered very attractive, I am naturally an object of suspicion amongst the local married women. I know there is a rumour going around in local circles that I'm supposed to be gay. I've done nothing to foster this, but neither have I gone out of my way to deny it. I find it takes the pressure off if they can pigeon hole me in some way. However, my looks still ensure that I'm frequently included on invitation lists, so I'm frequently meeting my masters outside of the disciplinary context.

There is a piquancy in maintaining a nice balance of friendliness and formality when out in public with a married man who, perhaps only a day or two before, had me hanging by my ankles while he whipped me between my legs as I sucked his cock. Him refusing to stop beating until I had sucked him dry, and me, if in a playful mood, not sucking hard at all, knowing he preferred my screams to my tongues caress. Or I may give way to the temptation to lightly bite instead of suck, and thus stimulate him to vicious revenge.

The anomalies imposed by this odd mixing of the private and public worlds can produce strains that need tempering by an understanding friendship. I am very fortunate that within a year of moving to Lincolnshire I met someone at a Whipping Party in Nottingham who I recognised as living in the same village as me! We became confidants, friends and then lovers, in a comfortably muted fashion. My friend is also a kind of submissive, but more of an observer than participant, so neither would or could stimulate me in the way I require. Our bedding is more friendly than fervent, the only kind of lover who not only doesn't object to my bruises and cuts, but is secretly pleased and excited about them. I have to say nice things about Jan. You see, I'm dictating this. It's actually Jan who's doing the writing. Thank you, Jan, darling! No, of course, that's not his real name. It's a joke between us. We share the same name, as we share so much else. It's another way we exclude reality from our private world!

Chapter 2: Libby

Age: 38, Location: North London, United Kingdom

Sadomasochism is in my blood. While some people may discover the more unusual sexual practices relatively late into adulthood as a result of a desire for more variety and experimentation and, perhaps, the generally more liberated outlook that comes with maturity, others have the feeling that their interest has always been with them; that it comes from within. I'm definitely in the latter category.

Somewhere along the line, as you grow up, you realise that certain things affect you in a certain way. Even before you have a proper awareness of sex and, in my case, definitely well before I'd ever had an orgasm, you find that particular images or ideas leave you with a slightly uncomfortable, yet strangely excited feeling. It's only later that you look back and realise it was because those images were related to the things you now find so arousing.

In my case it was scenes of chastisement, slavery or humiliation in films and books; like galley slaves being whipped to row faster, or the custom of some primitive tribes where all the women lie down in a row, by way of greeting, in order for male strangers to walk over them. Also, I was affected by (dare I admit it?) The whips and straps and enforced exertions of Black Beauty, which led to my interest in 'pony-girls'—a not uncommon branch of SM.

So, in the secret recesses of your mind, your fantasies develop and evolve, and a life-long interest is established. Nobody taught me or showed me or even suggested to me anything to do with SM. I just 'knew' that my sexuality revolved around male dominance of the female, and had no doubt about the fact that I identified with the sub role. It wasn't until I discovered through magazines in my early twenties that I realised my tendencies weren't unique and that other people were turned on by the same sorts of things. That, in fact, power games and ritualised submission of one person to another, combined with 'punishment', bondage and fetish clothing, represent just about the biggest 'alternative' sexual interest around.

In talking about my sexuality and submissiveness, I would have to distinguish between fantasy and reality. Of course, there are areas of overlap, but in general there's a big difference between the sorts of rather bizarre 'heavy' fantasies that go on in my head when I'm aroused and which help me to come, and the kinds of things I have actually done physically to myself, or would like to do, in real life. Let's deal with real life first.

I can't remember any one early experience that was a ground breaking 'first time', or that 'showed me the way' as far as SM is concerned. I was keen to experiment with sex, and seemed naturally to have a very liberated attitude. Most of my early experiences were driven by a more mainstream enjoyment of being with men, and lust for different partners. The other half of my sexuality, which is still very much a driving force in my life, is the idea of being very loose and available and, in particular, of being shared by more than one guy at a time. So the high points I remember most are some of those exquisite early threesomes I had, and all those absolutely gorgeous men (especially the foreign ones) who picked me up on my travels and enriched my life with their brief attentions.

Basically, I'd discovered in the course of my various encounters with different men the sorts of things I physically enjoyed and then made a point of encouraging and asking for those things whenever possible. And, yes, I liked to be fucked really rough; thrown down to the ground and pushed and yanked about. I like men to take what they want and to be demanding. I like to be forced onto my knees and told to suck cock. I like to be given specific instructions; told to wank, to turn over into a particular position or ordered to say something crude and inviting. I like to be spanked, and that's something you can ask virtually anyone to do, regardless of whether they're into the scene or not. I often suggest it when I'm with a group of guys, and there's always at least one who will happily oblige and seem to know what he's doing.

With several guys, you can also achieve some impromptu 'bondage', by having someone hold your arms and legs down, or up out of the way, while someone else has a go at your pussy or your mouth. I do love to be held down! A wonderful memory springs to mind of being with these two rather nice guys some years ago, in what developed into, if not strictly an SM session, an episode of serious male dominance. One of them straddling me across the chest, kneeling on my arms to keep them out of the way while the other took off his belt and began to pay some rather painful attention to my thighs and pussy. Oh, yes!

I can't say that I ever met any one, special man who was my 'perfect' master—and I haven't to this day. Though it's a significant part in it, SM hasn't become the whole of my life, as it does with some people. Maybe if somebody had come across me at the right time and known what to do with my potentially huge submissiveness. Things would have been different, but I've often thought that I couldn't really cope with a full-time master/slave relationship. In 'real' life I'm too independent, and there are too many other things I want to enjoy.

What I have done is seek out people who are keen to play the role of master with me. It doesn't matter too much to me who the man I'm submitting to is—it's what he does that matters. It's whether he understands how I want to be touched and spoken to, and whether I can achieve with him that wonderful, strict but playful rapport which makes SM sessions so fulfilling. It takes a little effort to find people on the same wavelength, and even at an early stage I was placing adverts, which is by far the simplest and most direct way to trawl society for those with a common interest. This has, undoubtedly, yielded some of the most interesting men and most 'formal', stylised SM sessions I've ever had. The trouble is that adverts also result, not so much in bad experiences, but in disappointing ones, and in some awkward and infuriating conversations with all sorts of people.

There are obviously lots of different interpretations of SM. Some guys think being sub means being passive—a doormat—and don't have any idea about creative play, and things like 'limits' and mutual respect. Others have an 'all or nothing' approach. I've even come across one or two who have refused to meet me and accused me of not really being submissive because I've indicated that there are certain things I don't want to do (like play with their girlfriends, for instance). There's also a lot of cases of dominance getting muddled up with arrogance—men who brag about all the things they've done. They come across as so sure of themselves and pushy, that they put you off immediately. And it seems that some people get off on power in a more unpleasant way—by deliberately messing you around, getting you to trust them, then walking out on you with a nasty comment, or pestering you with phone calls that intrude on other parts of your life.

In general, however, I've met dominant men who do and say the right things and are totally and utterly responsible and trustworthy. A girl just needs to hear a little reassurance about personal safety, and that nothing will happen that she doesn't want to happen. I've had some wonderful masters, men at whose feet you can't wait to throw yourself! Men whose leather or rubber clad bodies you can't wait to worship, whose delicious crotches you could rub your face against for hours. Men whose hands are as skilful with the ropes and straps as they tie you comfortably up in, as they are with the gentle manipulations of your pussy. Men who bestow sweet kisses when they pause from whipping you. Men who pull on your hair, whisper warnings in your ear, and pull your tits till they're sore. Men who push you to the ground with a foot at the back of your neck, and thrust huge dildoes up your holes and cane you till you weep, but who are always concerned for your comfort and safety. Men you can absolutely trust not to abuse the power you have temporarily given them. Men like the one I happen to have spent three hours with last night—a glorious hunk in layers of rubber, pressing me up against the wall of his little secret dungeon, and driving me onto an utterly escapist 'high' with his endless spanking and bondage and fucking!

I've also taught a few guys how to become more masterful—experimented with them, encouraging them to take the lead, and to say and do certain things. If it's not 'in your blood', then it does take a little learning, and it's great to watch people get more confident and start improvising on their own. And, recently, I've been going to fetish clubs where I virtually always get one or other (and usually more than one!) To play with me for a while. Largely because of this, I've had more spankings and whippings over the over the last two or three years than ever before. I do find myself playing the dominant role occasionally, but it doesn't really do anything for me—not in the deep emotional sense. The major plus point is that you get lots of licking and are in the position to issue instructions as to exactly how you like it!

So much for the joys and emotions of being submissive and playing sex games in the real world. I wouldn't be without it, and I've no intention of calling a halt to my activities yet. There still lots of limits to be explored and men to look up at and swoon over! But what about those heavy fantasies? I'm sure they're not unique, because I've read lots of 'literature' over the years that's along very, very similar lines, but how they are compared to the norm, especially where women are concerned, is hard to tell. Who knows what's going on in people's heads as they wank or fuck their way to orgasm?

Anyway, here's an idea of what goes on in mine. Bondage and 'women as objects' is one of the main themes. Women tied up in awkward positions and serving as pieces of furniture, for example. The woman that forms a chair, or footstool, or supports a coffee table on her back. Women as ornaments—standing like statues in recesses, immersed in the centre of a fountain in the garden, performing the function of a plant holder or a lamp stand, or draped across the middle of a table as an amusing centre piece.

I also enjoy strict and extreme bondage, tight rubber suits and restrictive body harnesses. Hobbles, handcuffs and tight corsets. Gags, blindfolds and collars that keep the head pushed back. Enforced physical activity, especially when in bondage (hence pony-girls), and—I can't miss it out—whipping! Prolonged, frequent and heavy chastisement, particularly on the back and ass, tits and cunt. I also fantasise about the idea of a whole society where women submit to men, where everything is geared up to men's pleasure, and where the women are perfectly happy to be of service. The details of the sorts of humiliating and degrading things women are expected to do, and the contrast between their suffering and the men's life f lei-sure. And, of course, the sexual use of women by men—lots of them at a time—and in all manner of outrageous and demanding circum-stances. I trust you'll understand that this sort of bizarre imagery doesn't condone or have anything to do with suffering and violence in the real world.

Well, there's lots more where that came from. My imagina-tion runs riot when it comes to sexual fantasy, but I'd better stop before I get carried away. I think SM is a fascinating and very com-plex part of the human experience and could do with being de-mystified in the eyes of the general public. I only know that it's not doing me any harm, and I'm very happy with it. I was just born to worship cock, I suppose!

Chapter 3: Anya

Age: 43, Location: Surrey, United Kingdom

Why is it infinitely easier to imagine such things than write about them? Is it the taboo nature perhaps? The very essence of the subject the reason for an inability to commit to paper. Just the thought of what I wish to write causes me to blush, although you have quite succinctly assured me you are unshockable. I do not for one moment think I will shock you; it is my suddenly acquired shyness that takes me by surprise.

I will start with some generalisations and hope I can ease more comfortably into some detail. I will have to say I am not into the schoolgirl/master thing that much. However, the authoritarian figure appeals, but I can't do the school uniform thing myself. Quite frankly, I feel ridiculous at the age of forty three, and it distracts from my being able to immerse myself into the moment.

As to corporal punishment, I am not into great pain barrier moments, but that can depend on the relationship and connection between the two people. The cane I am very sensitive to and anything more than gentle to mild tapping causes me to be nauseous. However, it could be used as a training tool as I don't like it at all; maybe one to be kept for later times, if things should progress to another level. As could be knives, of which I am absolutely petrified and would probably cause me to vomit if introduced inappropriately. I do not enjoy electrical gadgets of any kind.

I enjoy the heavy thuds of a suede switch, the warm hand being another favourite of course! I have one of those 'spikey' wheel gadgets which I particularly like and I have an especially sensitive spine. I like rope or leather cuff bondage, especially thigh cuffs, which for some bizarre reason make me feel more naked than being naked. Being 'made naked' is an especially delicious moment, which I like to savour, and causes me the most 'shame' Hence its deliciousness, I guess!

I enjoy being told what to do, given instructions and orders; the more explicit the more I enjoy them and dislike them at the same time. Being held by my hair is the sing-lest, simplest thing to elicit immediate submissiveness from me. I like the odd dildo or vibrator. Sometimes, however, vibrators have the opposite of the desired effect and numb the very places we are trying to stimulate! Being 'made to wait' for anything remotely pleasurable is a big turn on, too.

So where does this all come from?

My earliest memories of fuelling my masturbatory fantasies at the tender age of eight or nine consisted of twisted images I had contrived from the 'Colditz' type of Sunday movies my father favoured. In my fantasies these aggressive men with heavy boots and uniforms would have me tied naked to some kind of bed. One or two would appear to be 'in charge' and ordering others to tie me, undress me, move me into a more suitable position etc. Sometimes I would still have some clothes on and these would be removed carefully, savouring the moment of total exposure and complete with orders/commentary from the more senior present. One or more of them would caress me very slowly, until I orgasmed. This would in their minds exonerate them from torturing me as it 'proved' I enjoyed the treatment in reality, and related comments would bear this out. I was clearly a lowly British slut with no loyalty to my fellow countrymen if I should blatantly enjoy this treatment, and so on. As well as proving my slutness level, the imagined commentary accompanying this was that the junior soldiers doing the undressing/caressing would be 'preparing' for ease of entry into my body by the senior ones. I would then be forced to receive one or more of them at a time and then, at the same time, to perform fellatio against my will with whoever was thrusting into my mouth while holding me tightly by my hair.

All of my fantasies are variations on this theme and just at this very moment the thought of being over someone's knee, with my skirt being so slowly raised and my knickers being so slowly lowered, makes me wet and blush! That is one tiny element of the above, but is a very strong one.

I was introduced to the 'scene' by my best friend, Tim. I met him at a swinging party about eight years ago. We were both 'newbies' to that world. He was there with a very shy vanilla ex-girlfriend who had agreed to go 'exploring' with him, and I was there with my ex-partner (the father of my daughter) and, on reflection, trying to save a twenty year old relationship. I have to say I was not at all impressed with the swinging scene. It sounds as if it should be a delightful experience, but in reality is fraught with disaster and full of couples who are about to fall apart.

Tim and I hit it off as 'friends' straight away and, when my relationship took the final dive, he was the only one I could talk to about how and why it had gone pear-shaped. And I mean the only one. There had been stuff going on between me and the woman he left me for that I prefer not to talk about; it's so cliched, it's boring. We started going out socially together. His vanilla girlfriend wasn't interested in the scene. I, however, once recovered from the shock of my split, decided life was too short and wanted to investigate what the world had to offer and some of the things I had been thinking about for years.

We went to a fetish party in an old East End club that used to belong to the Kray twins, I think. I remember being absolutely petrified, but walked in and found myself thinking this is so comfortable. I have always been into clothes and dressing up; not in the fetish way, just generally, and this was like a big playground full of very polite, very nice people. I couldn't believe it. There wasn't anything going on between Tim and I at this time. We were still just good friends finding out what the scene was all about.

I can't remember the exact sequence of events, but around this time I started going out on the gay scene. It was absolute fun and madness. I had a great time and did some mad things, including setting up regular 'naughty lesbians' night at a club and taking part in saucy, but not outrageous, stage acts. During this time I met a woman I fell completely in love with. She still holds a special place in my feelings. I had an intense affair and, again, an amazing time. We had mad moments, too. Like, for instance, when she opened a restaurant in North London and I flew an outfit down from Scotland for her to wear at the opening. Our best times were going out on the town to very straight places, with me all glitzed up and girly and her, being a six feet tall K D Lang look alike dude, looking handsome in a tuxedo. We would love to do the 'romantic' couple thing and have these straight people in restaurants not being sure how to take it!

It was she, strangely enough, who gave me my first submissive experience. I can still visualise it to this moment. The next morning, she absolutely refused to discuss or acknowledge it, which was sad. This relationship fell apart for various reasons, partly due to my interest in the scene, and I moved on. I met another girl, who moved in with me and my daughter. We went out and about on the scene a little. It was good fun and I somehow ended up in the dominant role. One of my hottest scenes involves her; 'hottest', that is, in terms of exhibitionistic pleasure.

I then came to the conclusion I was not gay at all. I had been in love with the KD look alike because, quite simply, she was a man in a woman's body. She acted and behaved and was brought up to be an utter gentleman and it was that I was attracted to. I absolutely delighted in being 'her woman'. Around the same time, Tim discovered the Lady O Society, which caters for submissive ladies and dominant gentleman. Once I was single again, I joined as well. I had by this time been completely enticed by the submissive side of things and was turned on by the thought of wearing a collar and 'being some ones'.

We saw that a lot of Lady O members were trying hard to meet each other and, having no forum, we decided to start up a dining club; a safe and unthreatening environment for Submissives to meet dominants. That worked quite well and some of that group are now in my personal circle of friends and we still socialise and go out on the scene. By now I had got into some fetish reading material and decided I was ready to explore my submissiveness to the limits. I placed an advert in a magazine and had a fantastic response. One letter stood out completely from the rest. It made no reference to the scene at all, and was utterly charming and simply suggested meeting up for tea. Additionally, I had been studying handwriting and this revealed quite a lot. This was a pleasant person with a sensible approach to the matter. I was particularly impressed as many of the other letters that piled up were full of the 'do this, you slut' approach which, for a first contact, I thought was being a little optimistic!

For instance, I remember answering one advert in a scene magazine around this time. An unlisted phone number was given to me, along with instructions to call at a certain time, with which I complied. I was then told I would be sent a train ticket to Norwich. I said it was rather a long way to go for an introductory/exploratory meeting and suggested a neutral place for coffee or lunch somewhere between there and London. His reply was that, as I had mentioned I had, had some experience, I hardly needed to meet up to discuss things. I was simply told to come up to his house for an overnight stay. He then told me what he wanted to do to me. Presumably this was done in the hope that it would make me so horny I would jump on the next train. The scenario he had in mind was that he would tie me up and get his 'big black friend' in to fuck me while he watched. He would then beat me for being a slut. I said that I didn't think I could comply with that scenario without meeting him and forming some kind of relationship, and even then I wasn't one hundred per cent sure I would be able to. At this point he told me not to bother and hung up!

The worrying thing is that presumably some women just go "okay then see you next Saturday" or whatever. Going off to meet people you don't know and get involved in scenes straight away is the equivalent of playing Russian Roulette. The other thing that concerns me is the emotional fall-out of some of these women (submissive men too, I guess) who just run along and play without realising what can happen to them psychologically. Both parties are responsible though, and I often see adverts and letters in various places from 'wannabe' Doms who have no concept of safety, both physically or emotionally. I think, in general, they are 'vanilla' people who just stumbled upon the scene and thought it was an easy way to get sex, which is rather sad.

One of my colleagues has recently opened up about her situation and I'm trying to steer her away from the scenario she is in. Luckily her chap lives in the United States and doesn't get over very often, but he is one of those who has never been out on the scene, knows no other Doms, reads crap on the Internet and believes she should be a 'no-limits' sub. She is not allowed a safe word. He won't even allow her to discuss the issue, and doesn't give any comfort after scenes are over. She flew to the America to meet him and had a scene on their first meeting. Her first scene was with a home-made cat made from nylon rope! Now that's a very frightening person in my eyes and the kind that gives us all a bad name. Amazingly, it hasn't put her off all together and I'm going to take her out on the scene here, starting off gently with maybe a small club event. Then she can see for herself there are some sensible nice people out there who actually want her to enjoy herself as well as themselves.

I can't say I've seen or heard of any subs putting themselves in stupid situations apart from those incidents. In general, the people involved in the scene are pretty responsible. Okay, we've all maybe let a scene go a little further than it should, or had unfortunate mishaps, but the swinging scene is another matter altogether. Christ, you wouldn't think Aids ever existed, let alone any other disease that might be around. For instance, I know two women who are very into that scene. Both just love to take on as many guys in a night as they can. One has a penchant for black guys in particular, and in the times I've been out and about with them, a condom was never seen! There I'm off my soap box now!

Anyway, getting back to what I was saying earlier, I met up with the guy who had written the really impressive letter and, after several months, we started quite a serious sub/dom relationship. I soon became completely immersed in the relationship, was completely in love and it stayed that way pretty much for four years. Although during that time I sometimes went out and about and was playful with my friends, I was faithful and obedient! We mainly played in private, but had some time out and about on the scene as well. The first two years were absolute heaven and completely suited my lifestyle. At the time as I was running two businesses, a home, trying to cope with a mortgage on my own, bringing up an angry eleven year old and generally having to be in control of everything. To have those times of giving up control and decision making or thoughts of any kind was a complete and much needed release. Additionally, he completely spoilt me. If he liked to see me wearing a particular thing, he would go out and buy it. Things would arrive in the post beautifully gift-wrapped. Part of his pleasure was that shopping experience, with the staff of smart London stores knowing the gifts were not for his wife—a complete egotist! I had cards, letters and phone calls virtually every day.

As I began to recover myself and have time to 'fall in love', I found I wanted more in terms of time spent together. Needless to say, he was wrapped up in a 'proper' relationship elsewhere and it was never to be. At about the same time, we moved our relationship on to other planes and I began to play the dominant role. This also gave me the freedom to test the waters and meet other people. This was when I was tentatively looking around for another dominant figure in my life, but I could never get further than just being social and then running back.

Alongside all this, Tim and I had expanded our organising side of things to gathering people in unusual locations for parties. These were great fun and aimed mainly at the fetish crowd and, latterly, for the swinging crowd. I can't say my impression of the swinging scene improved any over the years. I used to think I didn't like it because I had been in love with the person I was supposed to be 'swinging' with, but I realised in the end that I just didn't like it in general! Occasionally it works very well and can be extremely erotic, but on the whole I find it distasteful and tacky—let alone dangerous!

During the period where we were organising our own fetish parties, one particular evening comes to mind which probably encompasses the most outrageous thing I have ever done. Not that it was particularly outrageous by fetish scene standards, but just by mine. Even now I can't believe I was this bold! Ours were not particularly devoted to sub females and dominant males, they were more of a mix. I think we were lucky at the time. It was strictly 'invite only' and if new people came along they had to be recommended by someone else in the group who had been to another event at the same time as the new people. That meant they could vouch for their sensible attitude, their discretion and their ability to socialise outside of the scene without being embarrassing. These were all qualities we looked for in our party attendees. This seems to have been the thing that made it work well, plus the fact that we weren't running it on a commercial money-making basis by letting less desirable people in. I think that is the main downfall of many clubs. Again, because of how carefully we let people into the group, we had a natural integration of people who could have fun and were never dangerous.

This is where I did my most extreme scenario which I mentioned before. We had a party in a private house owned by a friend of mine. It's a delicious house, glass-walled front and back, and located on an island, with the main room overlooking a river. It has a glass staircase going up the middle of a huge room leading to a glass landing. A stunning venue for naughtiness! When we took it over for the party, we dressed a small gallery overlooking the main room with red satin. We lit candles all around the bottom of the glass walls and draped some areas that were not conducive to the atmosphere. We had roses scattered on the glass floor of the landing and put some provocative classical music on. We also had a smoke machine delivering a floaty fog across the entire floor. There were two pieces of serious dungeon equipment installed.

The guests met in a local hostelry. They were then brought en masse to the bridge to the island. The subs were then blindfolded. We walked them across the bridge in single file to a small wooded area, then over another bridge which crossed a weir. The deafening sound of rushing water was an interesting sound effect for the blindfolded ones! We then arrived at a small grassy clearing, where the subs were ordered to remove shoes and walk across to the house. This time on damp grass—another interesting sensation! They were then led up onto a low deck where you step down into the house, right into the most incredible mist from the smoke machine and back lit by candles at the other end of a totally funky eighty foot long living space! The subs were then allowed to remove their blindfolds. The whole effect was fab! Some subs actually refused to go over the bridge that crossed the weir. But they all reported later that entrance to the party was the best they had ever experienced.

Once everyone was settled and coats dealt with and wine poured, they were treated to an erotic dance performed in the red satin lined gallery; another well received touch which set the mood completely. Food, buffet style, was served and socialising and play soon commenced. As I was co-hosting and it had been a quite stressful set-up, taking a few weeks to plan and all day to 'dress' the house, I wasn't completely dressed for play myself—that would come later!

I had, had a falling out 'ish' with my 'master' (with whom, by this time, I had been 'switching'), but he was coming along in a sub role for this particular evening. I had been upset as he had been trying to date my ex-lesbian lover and was being very insistent. He had (probably still has) a complete obsession with wanting to eat her pussy, and I was especially upset when he sent her a more expensive set of undies than me when it had been my birthday! Bastard! She, however, would never capitulate on the grounds that she was completely gay and this frustrated him no end!

Once he was into role I told him she was coming to the party and that she was willing to be sub for the night! He was devastated because being in sub role himself, he could do nothing about it! She was brilliant in her role. She arrived and did the 'sub' thing over the bridge and so on. He was completely fooled. Then she and I went upstairs and changed into our 'stomping boots' outfits, came down the stairs and called him over. He looked up and realised what was going on. I'm not sure if he was mostly frightened or excited. It was a really true mixture of both, as he had never seen me in revenge mode before.

We commenced a fairly heavy scene on a 'seat-cross' with whipping, cutting, play piercing and 'sewing', which was a particular penchant of his and which works very well visually in public. Then we took him to a 'floor-cross' that was very low down, about stool height. I had him rigged up in a mask with a cock gag. I then fitted him with this amazing steel cylinder contraption that encases the balls and has a 'screw-on' plunger that pushes up inside the cylinder. It's a fab piece of engineering and quite uncomfortable, as well as very heavy. I then proceeded to 'ride' his face while my ex-lover fucked his arse with a strap-on and whipped him some more. Then we called the dancer down from the balcony where she had been watching. She was at first quite hesitant to join us as this was not her scene. She was, after all, an erotic dancer, not a fetish player. I quickly did a visual check on Tim to see if he thought what I had in mind was a good idea. He okeyed it and so I ordered her down with instructions to obey me absolutely. I ordered her to remove her undies (she was by now dressed in a suitably submissive outfit) and I made her fuck herself with the cock gag while I kissed her passionately. Incidentally, she hadn't been kissed by a woman before either. My sub's eyes through his mask were ecstatic when he realised he was about to get as close a view of her pussy as you can get, so I quickly covered the eye holes. Needless to say, he was not a happy bunny! The dancer had a nice time though! Meanwhile, I peed into a wine glass and asked him if he was thirsty. He nodded yes, so I replaced the gag with a funnel and asked my, by now, unbelieving audience what they thought. We got the 'thumbs up' and gave him my nice warm drink.

We decided we needed a break at this point, so we let our 'toy' relax for a while and had some drinks. Then we decided we girls would like some more fun. We took him upstairs and made him kneel at the foot of the bed, cuffed with arms behind him. She and I then proceeded to have a most delicious time. I even let him taste my fingers, all sodden with her pussy juice. I still chuckle when I remember the forlorn look in his eyes. God, even now I think I should feel guilty for that evening, but I can't bring myself to. I'm sure he loved it all really.

I have to say, from my point of view, the evening had a very nice ending. Much later, when we had rested, we revived for a short while and I received a fab fucking by the girl with the strap on, laying on the bed with my head hanging off the side sucking him as submissively as you can get, while he stood and watched. Ah well. Once a sub always a sub, I guess!

In my own sub/dom relationship, I quite enjoyed the dominant role as well, as you can see. But it was taking over the times we spent together and although, on the face of it, I was adopting a dominant role, I was in fact still being submissive and giving him what he wanted! This became difficult between us and, as well as getting fed up with that, I was starting to yearn for a stable full-time relationship. I made a huge effort to extract myself from the relationship and look for someone who could fulfil me in all ways. I soon became disillusioned by the scene and what and who was available, so I turned my back on the whole thing and gradually dropped out altogether.

Chapter 4: Joy

Age: 27, Location: Essex, United Kingdom

My first insight into what I know now as my predestination to slavery took place when I was 19 years old. I had gone to a book sale and found a copy of 'The Story of O'. To this day I have no idea why I bought the book in the first place as it certainly was not my usual choice of reading material, but buy it I did. I found that over the coming days it became increasingly harder to put the book down and concentrate on everyday life. In many ways I envied O. It was obvious her submission gave her solace and pride, love and no fear of retribution or accusation. I found no cruelty in the book, nor did I find hate nor unhappiness, but it was not something I could discuss with my family nor friends, and so the book was put away and although never forgotten it was to spend the next 20 years as a distant memory of one the most beautiful books I had ever read.

On the whole my life from childhood to my late 30's was happy and full of fun. I dated and worked hard at establishing my own interior design and decorating business. Through cancer at the age of seventeen I found I would never know the joys (or should that be trials and tribulations!!) Of motherhood. Marriage was not something I would enter into lightly, thus I did not marry until I was thirty eight. It lasted only five years. My now ex husband was a violent man, a drinker and gambler, something he kept well hidden until after we married. And so in September 1999 I decided that no longer would I be an emotional and physical punch bag for a weak and gutless man. Divorce was inevitable. It was during the first days of my separation that my oldest and best friend came to stay with me, this was the first turning point in my mundane, empty life.

"To look after you, someone to listen to you and not to judge you". Beth had said. And in those first few days I had discovered that the things that had for years so often filled my mind were not wrong or bad, they were completely normal. And so, with the help and support of my friend, I began to find myself. I needed to know everything, constantly asking questions. Delving and searching, it all began to piece together. I knew where my path was to go and where my true destiny lay, that my life was to be one of a slave. These thoughts, this knowledge did not frighten me, I welcomed the day, when like Beth, I would kneel before my own Master and offer him my heart, mind, body and soul as his to do with as he saw fit. We talked for hours and I learnt something that was to change my life forever. Beth had for the whole of the thirty years I had known her been a submissive and yet I had no idea. Maybe this was because of my naivety and innocence (I had only had two lovers at this point) but never the less I was soon to have a true understanding of the real me that for so many years had been locked away and hidden deep inside of me. And so I began to take the first few faltering steps into a life that had for so long been denied to me. As a somewhat shy and nervous person I was not going to go in head first. I needed to know that this was not some romantic dream nor story book ideal I felt inside. I would not hurry to seek a Master nor Mistress. I had, had no bisexual experiences and at this time I would not have considered myself bi-curious but that was not to say this would always be the case, I tried hard to keep an open mind and not to judge others for their sexual or lifestyle preferences. I was soon to see I had a lot to learn.

So the journey along the path to my true nature began. Through Beth I was introduced to some wonderful people that I can now count on as my friends. In the early days, some could even be called my mentors. None tried to either influence nor push me, and many valuable lessons were learned! I went to munches, meetings and spent time reading books such as "The Loving Dominant", "Screw The Roses, Send me the Thorns" and "The Story of O", was taken from its resting place and this time it seemed even more beautiful than the first time I read it. Then, in September 2000, some friends from the USA visited the UK and this gave me a perfect opportunity to visit a lifestyle orientated club as they had offered to accompany me to a BDSM club in London called "The Gate". It was here I had my first glimpse of the man who was eventually to become my Master. I can still vividly remember seeing him this first time and new feeling washed over me. I felt myself grow warm, my breathing became faster and deeper, and at that point all I wanted was to go and throw myself at his feet and beg him to take me as his slave. It would be two years before my dream would become reality, and in that time not once did I feel differently.

Those next two years passed slowly. It was as if my life was in limbo. I still visited various BDSM style clubs, met even more people and learnt during this time there was no shame in being a slave, so at last I could live my life. I discovered that so many people live their lives being something that in reality they are not. We tend to hide our true self and our sexuality under a cloak of darkness because we are either to frightened or too ashamed to be ourselves and live as we really wish. As I saw it, my life was now going where it should be, but with one thing missing—a Master. And the question still remained how was I going to approach Master Keith and offer myself to him? In the end it was easy! I knew by October 2002 that he no longer had a collared slave and so I took a deep breath and emailed him! A few days later, whilst I was at work, he called me. We chatted easily and I was invited to visit him with a view to helping him host The Gate Club. Later that evening I drove to his house and we talked nearly all night. It was apparent there was an attraction between us, one that was soon to prove impossible for me to walk away from. I was in his eyes still a very inexperienced newbie. After all, he had been practising BDSM for thirty years and I had only discovered this wonderful, but so often misunderstood, lifestyle some three years previously. To Master Keith, this of course would not present a problem, for I was malleable and could be trained in exactly the way he wished. One question however remained firmly fixed in my mind—would he want me, could I be all he wished as his most prized possession?

If he accepted me as his slave, I knew that I would do whatever it took. Never had I met a man with such an aura of control. Sheer animal sexuality poured from him like a river that has burst its banks. He was magnetic. I was drawn so strongly to him that the nights I spent away from him were lonely and empty. I had fantasised about him taking me, whipping and using me, and controlling every aspect of my everyday life. I wanted him to own me and I needed to belong to him. In essence he was rapidly becoming the most important thing in my life. Already everything I did, and the things I thought, revolved round what would make him happy. At last, I too was happy and content and very soon I would truly understand what fulfilment really meant.

The next few weeks flew by. Master Keith had designed a plastic chastity belt that was to be sold under the name Love Locks, and there was much to do for the advertising and web site that was under construction. I wore one quite often. Plans were also under way for a male version, They were comfortable, hygienic and had more use than just a chastity belt as I found out once or twice. Master had also formed one with a hole under the vaginal opening, into this hole he placed a pump up type dildo. The pipe was placed outside the belt through the hole and so could be pumped up on a whim. If he went out and left this in place by the means of a combination type padlock, unless I knew that combination, I was powerless to remove it. December was upon us before I even realised it. The beginning saw the re-launch of The Gate Club, and with it my first time out in public as my new and real persona. In some ways it was frightening and yet also edged with a hedonistic excitement. I felt so proud to be knelt at Master Keith's feet, or to be stood at his side. That night when he led me to the play room area and bid me to lay across the spanking bench I thought my heart would burst, I drifted quickly and easily into his world, he carried me higher and higher. I was spinning into a vortex of colours I had never seen the like of before.

His hands scorched and burnt my bottom, while his calm resonate voice clouded my senses and calmed my fears. I was naked and vulnerable in front of people I had never met before. My cleanly shaved pussy on view to any that cared to glance in our direction, and if I found that was embarrassing what happened next was mortifying to me. Deftly his fingers parted my pussy lips and his fingers delved inside me. Swiftly he brought me to a mind blowing orgasm that seemed to go on for ever. All I could think of at this time was my first encounter with this man. My aching rear and tenderised sex constantly reminded me of him for seven days after we had met. I let my mind mull over the memory, licking it like a lollipop and relishing in its sweet taste.

Was it really only eight weeks ago that I had come willingly to the man that was to change my life forever? So powerfully had he stood in front of me that my breath was wrenched from my slight frame as he smiled a slow lazy smile that entered my body like a tidal wave. I am not by any means a girl, and yet I blushed profusely in the company of this daunting man. I felt his strength and power and could do nothing to pull my eyes from his. Although by now I was not that new to the lifestyle, I was still fairly innocent. I had never taken or demanded anything life had to offer me. I had known I was somehow not complete or whole and I knew also that the person I had portrayed for so many years was not the real me. It was at the end of this night he finally agreed to accept me as his slave. A contract would be drawn up and agreed upon by both parties. A list of the rules I was to always obey would be discussed and also agreed, and it was decided that I would now move in with Master Keith and my training would begin. My official collaring would take place on February 21st 2003 in front of friends that would act as witnesses as I gave myself to him into a life of slavery. On the journey home in the early hours of the morning I was euphoric. He made me laugh, captivated my total attention and when we finally parked the car and he bade me to follow him and go to the dungeon and remove the few clothes I was wearing I nodded almost shyly and followed him meekly from the car. The next few hours passed in a blur. Slowly and deliberately I removed the few garments and dropped them in a pool at my side, only when I was totally naked did he stand and walk around me, occasionally reaching out and stroking my soft skin. At his touch I nearly dropped to my knees, it was electric. I knew from that time on I would refuse him nothing. When he told me to kneel at his feet, I did so willingly. Neither did I cry out or flinch as he laid into my arse with the tawse, nor complain when he took me brutally some hours later. And how proud I felt when later that same morning with his eyes twinkling he whispered into my ear." So you want to be my slave?" Now here I was, entering a new world!

I would never doubt him, for he is honesty personified. He is my truth. He allows me to lull into a soft fantasy where I am once more under his attentions. The feel of him sliding his fingers into me, of ravishing me, tying me, commanding me, whipping me, all of it plays often through my mind's eye. Those wonderful, intense mind-blowing moments when he unleashes symphonies of pleasure and quivering orgasms that have me writhing on the bed clawing at the sheets, My mind so often filled with the images that were still so vibrant. How he helps me to gain strength for my journey ahead. The feeling of euphoria from being set loose in such a distinctly dissimilar place, elevating me into a heady joy. It is as though I am dreaming; walking in a land conjured by my own wandering thoughts. It is through him a sense of preternatural freedom surrounds me. An air of being separated from all consequences of my actions due to my knowledge of not having to live with outcomes kindles a sort of criminal instinct. A mischievous whim that my own sense of decorum and morality kept subdued. It was not a desire to commit some sort of felony, but a childlike eagerness to misbehave, to act and do things I felt myself unable to do before because of the stifling choke hold wrought by friends and family. To be free of these encumbrances is wonderful. I am free and yet not free, for he owns me. I had already offered myself to him and he had accepted me, taken me as his property, but I still feel this sense of freedom. I can express myself as I really am. And what greater freedom could I have than knowing I please my Master? That I am his most prized and valued possession.

The weeks leading up to my collaring did not actually pass uneventfully either. I knew my life as slave to Master Keith would at times be hard and daunting, and I was soon to find out that punishment was not something I would relish nor look forward to. The day had started as it usually did. I arose and went straight to make Masters coffee and check his post and emails. I filled his bath and helped him to bathe, dried him and dressed him. We had breakfast together and the usual household tasks were completed by just after lunch. That day Master had a visitor. I knew I should not raise my voice nor make displeasure known in company, but acting totally out of character I was childish and selfish. Master on the other hand merely raised his eyebrows at my outburst and quietly told me that he would deal with me later. By 7pm he still had not mentioned the events of earlier, I had cooked his evening meal and tried hard in my own way to appease him for my actions earlier in the day, but he had not forgotten. Soon after this he reminded me that I had misbehaved and that punishment was inevitable. He bade me to fetch his tawse and cane and to go to the dungeon and await him. This I did immediately and without question. I slowly walked down the steep stairs and did as he asked, kneeling at the bottom of the stairs, my eyes lowered not only from respect but from a deep penetrating regret that I had displeased him. Soon I heard his footsteps. My heart was beating so loudly I was sure he could hear it, but if he did no reference was made. He grasped my wrist and pulled me to my feet and led me over to the whipping bench. I was told to lay myself over it and quietly he explained that he was most certainly going to punish me hard. He informed me it was not a chore he was looking forward to but one that would none the less take place and that he hoped something that would not become a regular reoccurrence.

He bound me tightly that night. My wrists and ankles were cuffed and a strong leather belt pulled firmly across my middle. I knew then that he was not joking nor kidding with me. I felt my skirt being lifted and my buttocks felt a chill of ice. I wondered briefly at that moment if he was going to spank my bare arse, but before the thought was even fully formed I felt the sting as his hand came firmly down on my cheeks and a quick succession of similar blows rained down until my arse was well and truly tingling and most decidedly warm. I squirmed and wriggled as best I could under my bonds throughout the onslaught. In the mirror I saw him reaching down. He picked up a riding crop and swatted each buttock six times sharply. The pain was acute, and tears shone in my eyes betraying my inner turmoil. And in Master's gaze I caught sight of the glimmering light shining on the lake of sadism. It was a look I had not seen in him before. I shivered as I accepted in advance the burning promises of that gaze. Minutes later he gagged me and used the tawse and cane on my arse. Then he left me bound and gagged, alone and shivering. The sobs racking my body. I was being given time to reflect on the events of the day. I was so deep in thought I did not hear Master return, but I felt his hands releasing me from the whipping bench. He stood me before him and put his arms tightly around me and held me to him, all the time speaking quietly and telling me that it was now finished. It would not be mentioned again and that he took no pleasure at all from punishing me. I felt so ashamed, and I hurt. The pain from the whipping was acute, but not so acute as the pain I felt in my heart that I had displeased Master and in turn had caused him distress at having to punish me. He led me quietly from the dungeon, tears still falling from my eyes. Leading me to the bedroom he kissed me gently and told me to wrap up warmly. It was now 11pm, the night before it had snowed and that snow still lay on the ground. He smiled and told me we were going off tobogganing! Proof indeed that this Master was compassionate, fun and strong. To this day he has never once mentioned that night, but in my heart I still feel the pain from my misdeed.

January quickly turned into February, and everyday Master Keith was proving to be all I could ever wish for in a Master. His patience was relentless, his energy unfailing, his mind evilly, devilishly demanding. Before I knew it the twenty-first was upon us. Every few days he had asked me the same question, whether I wanted to be his slave and every time without question my answer remained the same—YES! And so, with the guests assembled, I knelt before

Master Keith and looked up confidently as I offered myself to him as his slave. I trust him with my life, in everything, every decision, and every deed. I gave myself in submission to him, my heart, soul, body and mind. All I am I gave to him freely and without question nor fear. I wear his collar with pride and honour, his ring with love and chastity. I live only for him and his pleasure and obey him always and without question. I do these things because I want to, not because he has demanded it. How much tenderness and love I feel for my Master. How well he understands me. His whips have provided the explanation I have sought all my life. I have surrendered myself to him because I was fated to be captive, destined to find all my pleasures in my submission. He has given to me my true self, and my true place is here with him. From now on I await his return steadfastly, always groomed, as naked or clothed as he decrees, ready for each act of indecency and even instigating it. How cheerfully I now rise above my woes. Safe and loved and cherished by my beloved Master. I remember often the first evening I saw him and how I had replied when he had asked me what I saw in myself. I had answered that I am conscious of my nothingness, of my dark shadows. I am spurred on not by pride, but by the desire to know where the truth lies and how to reach it. And now I know, I have found my truth, I have found it in Master Keith.

Chapter 5: Christine

Age: 34, Location: United Kingdom

I was first introduced to open air exhibitionism by my Master (later my husband), David. Ever since I was a young girl in my teens my fantasies have revolved around the idea of being exhibited and sexually used by groups of men. In my dreams they didn't even have to be handsome studs, often the thought of being fingered and groped by dirty old men would turn me on terribly. As with most sexual fantasies, they remained just that, safely tucked away in the further most recesses of my imagination until I began a sub/dom relationship with David. Being 15 years older than me (I was 22 when we started going out), I found he had sufficient experience and understanding of my needs to bring me out of my shell. Younger lovers would have been too judgmental and possessive to help realise my potential for erotic exploration.

Most importantly, for a woman, I always feel safe and completely protected. And because he is such a control freak and so naturally dominant, he takes pleasure in allowing other men to play with me and then stopping the action when he chooses. No man would argue with my Master when told to back off, no matter how far gone they were with lust.

I remember the very first time my Master placed me in a 'situation'. It was completely unplanned—well, at least on my part—during a hot sex session in a local park. We were getting down to it in a secluded wooded area when David whispered in my ear that we were being watched. To my horror (I'm quite a prude, sometimes!) I realised a young guy was furtively ogling us from a few yards away. My shock was compounded when I saw he had his jeans and pants lowered and was masturbating for all he was worth. I instinctively made a move to fasten my bra and retrieve my panties when David took hold of my wrist and reminded me firmly that this is what I had always wanted to happen and now I was getting my wish. I squirmed and pleaded that I had changed my mind but David would have none of it. Shutting me up, he forced my legs wide apart to allow our audience an uninterrupted view of my cunt.

As David fingered me to a mounting excitement, he smiled over at the fellow to let him know that his voyeurism was quite acceptable. Out of the corner of my eye I could see the young man pluck up the courage to start walking towards us. Despite the state I was in, I remember finding the sight of him hobbling towards us while trying to keep his trousers up with one hand and continue with his wanking with the other quite hilarious. However, the smile was soon wiped off my face when I noticed a second figure emerge from cover to our right, similarly exposed and masturbating.

David, however, was completely unperturbed and, knowing he had done this sort of thing with previous girlfriends, put me at my ease. As I said earlier I had absolute trust in him as my protector, otherwise I'm sure I would have run or screamed. The first guy was even younger than me and, as he drew closer, I realised to my delight that he was a very well endowed boy indeed. The second was a much older man, probably in his late fifties, and reminded me of my headmaster at school, which in itself was an added buzz. The contrast between the two was very exciting for me. In my fevered imagination it was almost as if I was about to be used by a father and son together!

Master David was wonderful, of course. He completely stage managed the proceedings with the consummate skill of a theatre director, telling each of them what they were allowed to do whilst positioning me how he wanted. First, he ordered me to kneel so I could suck both men in turn, while they fondled my breasts. Again I was turned on by the difference between the two of them. The young cock was very thick, hot and hard. The second was smaller and only semi-erect despite my furious sucking. The older guy did, however, have one distinct attraction in that he possessed the biggest pair of balls I'd ever experienced! Next, I was told to position myself doggy-style for a good fucking from both ends. David produced condoms which he made the younger guy put on before entering me. Then he knelt before me so I could suck on his own marvellous cock at the same time. The 'headmaster' was really getting into it, too. He lay on his back and wriggled himself underneath me so he could play with my dangling boobs. At the same time I was able to reach out one hand and give those lovely monster balls a good feel!

After I had been pumped full of their seed and all four of us had come, I was amazed at how easily the two were dismissed by my Master. The young guy turned surprisingly shy and sheepish and simply mumbled thanks to David before shuffling off, presumably to find some more action elsewhere. The other, older man, was obviously more experienced in this sort of thing and had probably been doing this sort of thing for years. He thanked David profusely for my use and affectionately patted my bottom in farewell.

When we arrived home. I was still on a sexual high and couldn't wait to be used again. Since that day my wonderful Master has exposed me to many wide and varied experiences. I've been used in saunas, sex cinemas and by the seaside. Even in gents public toilets! However, my favourite is still the woods. We have been back to that first spot many times and still feel the same thrill of the unknown and the dangerous every time we arrive at the car park and walk past all those hungry guys all watching me and wanking furtively and me not knowing which will be using me this time! I hadn't even realised such scenes existed and even less aware that I would be married to a man who was well acquainted with the whole network that exists for enthusiasts of outdoor group sex. It has certainly been an eye-opener! Recently we have introduced another female to our games. Joanne is a divorcee in her mid-forties who is submissive and bisexual. As Master David's second slave we have embarked on even wilder adventures which, if my Master allows, I will write about another time!

Chapter 6: Lorraine

Age: 37, Location: Surrey, United Kingdom

My fantasies have always every time around sacrificial scenarios—with me, of course, as the more than willing victim! Sometimes, in my dreams, I am in Ancient Mexico being sacrificed to the gods by half naked, feather bedecked Aztec priests on top of a pyramid and under a cruel, merciless desert sun. Other times, the scene is a secret coven of pagan witches and wizards who spread eagle me naked on a cold stone slab before using me in their potent fertility rites.

In fact, my fantasies can get quite, well, fantastical! Like the time I am on another planet being examined as a scientific curiosity by alien professors. Even wilder; my tormentors are not even human, but many-tentacled triffid-like plants, prodding and probing my naked body.

Whatever the scenario, the main erotic ingredient that is ever present is the ritualistic element. There is always a definite theatrical structure to the proceedings that I need to totally involve me. Also, my masters/tormentors (the more the merrier, as far as I'm concerned!) Are always masked or hooded like executioners or medieval inquisitors to give them a frightening, dispassionate anonymity. No one speaks, apart from my master who may issue occasional instructions to the men. After all, they all know their roles in our erotic pantomime.

Above all, I am not informed of what I am letting myself in for at any session, nor am I given a choice in the matter. My present

Master, Matthew, works on the assumption that if a scenario excites me as a fantasy, then there is no reason he shouldn't 'force' me to do it for real. Looking back, I realise that if I had not been forced into situations without any option for refusing, I would probably still be the sheltered, naïve little housewife I was when we first met.

Perhaps I should explain the whole situation of our relationship at this point. You see, my Master is also my boss. I started working as a part-time typist and receptionist for his company two years ago. It wasn't long, however, before we realised our mutual interests and began an affair. My office duties now take on a very different meaning as you can imagine!

Anyway, this cover works perfectly for our regular 'get-togethers'. My boss/master can ring me at home at anytime when he wants me without arousing my husband's suspicions. I know I am a filthy slut, but I must admit I get incredibly turned on and excited if my husband takes a call from Matthew and relays the message in all innocence that I have to be at 'work' at such and such a time. The fact that only I know the true meaning behind the summons is very erotic to me.

If I answer the phone while my poor, unsuspecting hubby is in the room, Master Matthew will invariably take a cruel delight in giving me very explicit instructions about how I am to dress when I present myself for his pleasure and what sexual acts I will be expected to perform. As he talks dirty I have to maintain a business-like pretence, answering his lurid suggestions with "I'm sure that can be arranged" or "I don't see any problem with that" or some such innocuous reply.

The heady cocktail of guilt, intrigue and danger gets me tremendously excited even before he's laid a hand on me. Added to this the fact that I'm actually being paid an hourly rate by his company for all this (which is more than Monica Lewinsky was!) Makes me feel a real horny whore.

On one particular occasion my husband had taken the call while I was out screwing another lover (but that's another story; not even my Master knows about that one!). When I got home I was feeling well-fucked and (I thought) fully satisfied. But when hubby informed me that Matthew had called saying he had some 'very important' clients coming for a meeting the following Tuesday evening and he needed me to offer hospitality I knew that this was going to be the big one I had fantasised about! As far my poor, deluded spouse was concerned the job meant nothing more than making the sandwiches and serving coffee. I, however, was under no illusion that the only tasty morsel being served on the menu would be my naked body! Master Matthew knew all about my desire to experience a group of men together in a sacrificial scenario and had promised to arrange it as soon as he was able to gather together a suitably qualified group of helpers.

I could hardly wait for Tuesday to roll around. As each day passed my fear and excitement grew in roughly equal proportion until my pussy was literally permanently buzzing like a dynamo in anticipation of being well-filled and well fucked. On the appointed evening, I prepared a dinner for hubby to eat in front of the TV. My son Jason wasn't interested in dinner. He was going out, he informed me. He was very evasive and blushed coyly when I inquired where. As he has just turned eighteen I assumed he must have found himself a girlfriend and let the matter drop. Adolescents have their own secret world that adults are not allowed to know about, I reflected as I popped upstairs to get ready for Matthew. Still, I found myself grinning mischievously to myself, teenagers are not the only ones with secret rendezvous!

When I arrived at my Master's house I was taken immediately into a side room off the main hall. From the adjoining lounge I could hear masculine voices talking and laughing. It sounded like four, maybe five men. They appeared to be having a party. My stomach churned in anticipation of an out and out gang bang. Suddenly, every instinct in my body wanted me to turn and run back to the sanctuary of my safe little home and cosy spouse.

Master Matthew sensed my trepidation and frowned reproachfully. Despite my fears, I was more worried about displeasing my master than what might happen to me. Above all, I wanted to prove to Master Matthew, and myself, that I was able to offer myself up to his will completely. He reminded me of the fact that he was only fulfilling the fantasy that had come out of my own imagination, not his. And that I wasn't being forced to do anything I hadn't previously admitted I wanted to do.

There was no point denying it. Master Matthew had wrung every last erotic fantasy out of me under his interrogation. And I knew well enough what his rules were. Any fantasy can, and will, become a reality. In a frightened whisper, in case the noisy party in the next room overheard me and I might cause embarrassment to my beloved master with my inexcusable insubordination, I dared to ask how many men were waiting to use me. He just smiled that cruel smile of his and, cupping my chin in his powerful hand, turned my face up to him and informed me there would be enough to satisfy even a cock hungry whore like me!

I needed desperately to know what I was letting myself in for. I felt I had to prepare myself mentally for the erotic ordeal I knew I must face, but I knew he wasn't going to tell me. Ignoring my silliness over numbers and details, my master wisely ordered me to remove my coat, knowing the act of stripping would always get me in the mood for sex. With trembling fingers I unfastened the buttons down the front to reveal my complete nudity beneath-as he had stipulated I should arrive.

I felt incredibly excited, as I always did, as I felt his lecherous eyes ravishing my body and his big strong hands took hold of my ample breasts, squeezing them just hard enough to hurt a little and then bouncing them appreciatively in his massive palms as he weighed them like a pair of ripe melons. Next, his fingers expertly traced a line down between my cleavage and belly, and then across the freshly shaved smoothness of my pubic mound and slipped easily into the moist crack of my pussy.

Exploring the hot wetness, he grinned knowingly, "So, you don't want this, eh? We both know your cunt has a different opinion, don't we, slut?"

I blushed with shame at this undeniable give away of my desires and tried to avert my eyes from his penetratingly, powerful gaze. My mouth was as dry with fear as my pussy was wet with excitement. It was these conflicting sets of emotions fighting against each other that addicted me to our games and made me return to my Master again and again.

The question was repeated with greater insistence, interrupting the delicious delirium caused by his fingers probing roughly inside me.

"Yes." I weakly admitted, feeling myself powerless to do anything but be completely honest about even my most filthy and disgusting sexual needs with my Master. Master Matthew then ordered me to take off my coat and hang it up. Enjoying the sight of me stark naked in the hallway.

"The hour of your sacrifice has arrived." My Master announced with grave, almost religious, severity. "This is your moment of truth where you must prove yourself and the faith I have put in you as my most treasured slave. You won't let me down?"

I assured him I wouldn't. I was so anxious to prove myself a worthy slave by pleasing all his dominant male friends. My failure to satisfy them all sexually, no matter what they might require of me, would reflect badly on him and their estimation of his ability to train a slave and bend her to his superior will.

Next he draped the black velvet sacrificial cloak around my shoulders, fastening it in place with a heavy gold locket so that my nakedness was completely hidden beneath the heavy shroud. Then he put the leather hood in place on my head so that only my eyes and mouth were revealed, thus assuring my absolute anonymity. "You know what you must do?"

As if I could forget! I had fantasised my way through the pageantry of this scenario a thousand times in my imagination already. But I managed to conceal my excitement and merely confined myself to a simple, "Yes, sir. I know what is expected of me and I will not fail you."

He smiled at me as a father would upon his favourite child. I felt a glow of satisfaction that I might yet become his most favoured sex slut.

"Come, girl." He said soothingly, as he led me to the living room door. He made me wait outside, head bowed, while he went ahead and announced my entrance to the waiting men. Through the closed door I could just discern the muffled voice of my beloved tormentor informing them that their entertainment was about to commence. There were murmurs and grunts of lewd animalistic approval that sent shivers down my spine and put butterflies in my belly.

Matthew emerged from the room, after what seemed an age and, just before he led me in to face my fate, whispered in my ear that, although I wouldn't know who, one of his guests was well known to me. It might be one of my work colleagues at Matthew's company; it might even be my husband or father, he suggested with an amused air and an evil chuckle.

This was so typical of my Master to add such a cruel twist at the last possible moment in order to spice up the proceedings even more. My mind was suddenly flung into even greater turmoil at the thought as I found myself guided into the centre of the lounge surrounded by Matthew's special friends. It was too late for regrets or retreat now. There were six of them in all, not including my Master. They stood, lining the edge of the room around me. Each had a drink in his hand, and some were casually smoking cigars as they eyed me in eager anticipation of seeing my nakedness revealed. It might have been a very normal get-together, except for the fact that, apart from their executioners style hoods that my Master had specified they should don, they were all stark naked and sporting rampant erections!

With great ceremony my Master slowly unbuttoned my cloak and took it from me, leaving me naked in full view of all these strangers. Instinctively, I modestly cast my eyes down to the floor while my left arm shot up in an attempt to cover my breasts and my right hand went down to hide my pussy from all those lecherous eyes. Then, catching the disapproving look of my Master, I remembered my place and my role. Letting my hands drop to my sides, I drew myself to attention, like a slave on an auction block, fixing my gaze firmly on the wall ahead of me and tried desperately to ignore those lust-crazed eyes fiercely feasting on my vulnerable nakedness.

Soft, sensual mood music started to play on my Master's sound system. I recognised it from our previous one-to-one sessions and knew exactly what was required of me. Slowly and seductively, I began moving my arms and body in time to the music. Losing myself in my erotic dance, I swayed and twisted like a shameless strip-tease artiste. I had been well trained to perform this way and my Master often said I was a very sexy dancer for my age with my still trim figure, tight buttocks and firm, bouncing boobs. The only trouble was I had only performed like this in front of one man before—not a whole group of wanking males!

Still, it didn't take long for me to get into my perverted solo performance, and quite soon I was showing myself off to them all with pretty wild abandon while they closed in on me from all sides like a pack of hungry animals for a group grope. Wriggling provocatively as a dozen hands touched me up, I thrust out my pert buttocks and spread my ass cheeks with my fingers to expose my arse and wet pussy for inspection. As their exploration of my body grew wilder and more intimate, I did my own bit of ogling at all the cocks on display. Safe behind my mask, I enjoyed myself by grabbing any cock that came within reach as they rubbed up against me. I then dropped to my knees for a 'circle-suck', as my Master calls it, and proceeded to take all their throbbing pricks in my mouth one after another. I was both amazed and delighted at the variety of shapes and sizes on offer. I was getting very carried away now, particularly with one young man whose fresh, sweet-tasting cock excited me more than some of the other men's members. Even with their faces hidden, I could tell most were late middle-age or even older.

At a given command from my Master the men scooped me up into the air. Quite without warning I found myself held high and helpless, like a coffin, on their shoulders. They carried me aloft, like pall bearers, and headed from the lounge with Master Matthew leading the way. Again, I was both thrilled and terrified that my fate was being decided for me and I had no idea what was in store for me now; only that I sensed the moment of my real sacrifice to the Gods of Lust had arrived at last!

The adjoining double doors were thrown open and I was borne on high by my prospective abusers into the Master's dining room—or what I remembered as a dining room! For this very special occasion Master Matthew had excelled even himself with his attention to erotic detail by transforming the space into a veritable temple of sacrifice. The curtains were drawn tightly closed and the dining table itself was covered in a black silk sheet, like a pagan altar. Around the darkened room ornate candles cast ominous shadows against the walls. Incense burned everywhere, adding a final, almost mystic touch to the scenario. I could feel my pussy juices flowing freely and my nipples hardening to rigid nuggets at the exciting, yet terrifying, prospect of what was to become of me and finding that I was already so consumed with desire that I didn't even care anymore!

Slowly, gently, my exquisite tormentors laid me out on the altar like a prize offering to their cruel, unforgiving God of Lust. Silently and expertly, they spread-eagled my arms and legs, pinning me down by wrists and ankles. In doing so they made sure that they positioned themselves in such a manner that my fingers could still grip a pair of the hard cocks offered me, while my toes were in intimate contact with two sets of testicles! Next, I was stretched wide as each man in turn went down on me, licking and sucking furiously at my soaking cunt. Then my master demonstrated his skill at abuse by introducing some very interesting objects into me. First, a dildo, then a candle, followed by a long stemmed wine decanter and, finally, his fist. I could tell by the appreciative noises being made around me that Master Matthew's guests were suitably impressed by his skills as a dominant, as well as my threshold for this kind of extreme abuse—thanks, of course, to the wonderful training my master had already given me. I felt a warm glow of satisfaction and achievement, knowing that I was proving myself a worthy asset to his harem.

When my master had decided he'd had enough of this phase of my abuse, he motioned for each man in turn to have sex with me, while the rest kept me pinned down and spread wide. One after another, I was subjected to a thoroughly rigorous fucking by each of the sweating, grunting and abusive elderly men as my master stood back and surveyed the scene of debasement, playing with his own cock all the while and urging the others on to use my 'whore's hole' with as much force as they could muster and not be dainty with me. Meanwhile, several score of frenzied fingers continued to grope and maul at me mercilessly as I kept up my teasing of their cocks and balls with my own digits to make sure I kept them all at full boil!

Naturally, I was paying particular attention to playing with the youngest man's tackle, which I was gripping firmly in my right hand. Without warning, his excitement at seeing a woman, who must be old enough to be his mother, acting the part of such a shameless slut before his eyes, got the better of him and he spunked furiously, spraying thick white streams all over my face and tits. Greedily, like some whore possessed, I began licking at the gobs of sweet tasting boy-spunk still dribbling out of his cock and down the lovely thick shaft of his purple headed monster. As well as enjoying the act tremendously, I also wanted to ensure he got hard again as soon as possible. I was determined I was going to have that cock exploding in my pussy before the evening was over. I also had a sneaking suspicion my Master had something lined up for me and this young, novice dominant. As it turned out, I was right!

Master Matthew had indeed got it all planned out for me, as I knew he would. At his command the men let go of me and stood back, leaving me for the young stud to pleasure himself with. The horny boy didn't waste any time in taking full advantage of the opportunity or of me! Grabbing me by the legs, he dragged me down the table to impale me on his already hard-again cock. Then he proceeded to give me the fucking of a life time while the others wanked over me. Without taking his delicious cock out of me, he somehow managed to clamber onto the table and on top of me. There was no stopping me now as I wrapped my legs round his waist, locking him in position, and grabbed his firm young buttocks, urging him to thrust harder and deeper into me. I was like a bitch on heat and determined to put on a really filthy sex show to impress my master's guests, as well, of course, as making sure I got as much mileage out of this succulent young man as possible. My hands and mouth were everywhere, scratching his back and sinking my teeth into his neck and shoulders, leaving him covered in love-bites. The thought of being a cradle snatching whore was really turning me on! After fucking my cunt in a variety of positions, Master Matthew told him it was time to give my ass-hole the same treatment. Accordingly, my young lover withdrew his cock for a moment and, flipping me over, proceeded to ram himself into my arse right up to the hilt, at the same time reaching round to maul at my tits very roughly. There was no respect from this lad for a mature lady old enough to be his mother, which is just the way I wanted it!

He came several more times as we fucked on that table. Once in my ass hole, and another time in my cunt. Counting the first time I'd taken it in my mouth, that meant I'd had his spunk in every orifice. In addition, the other men, inspired by our antics, all shot their respective loads over me till I was covered in the hot, sticky stuff. Eventually, I wore out all their cocks and Master Matthew instructed them to pick me up again and carry me to the bathroom where I was to have the spunk washed off me in a most unconventional manner! Once there, I was ordered to kneel in the bathtub while each of the men took turns to hose me down with a good, hard pissing! Again, my master decreed that my young stud should have the honour of finishing the group urination with something special for their entertainment.

While the others gathered eagerly around to see what was about to happen, Master Matthew ordered the young man to stand in front of me and to, in his own cruel words, 'give the whore a drink'. I knew what this meant as it was one of the master's favourite ways of abusing his women. He produced a funnel, which he handed to the boy with instructions to shove it down my throat. For the first time I sensed some hesitation in the poor young chap which, I must admit, is a bit of a turn-off for any submissive woman. But I put it down to his youthful inexperience, and reckoned that with my master's expert guidance and encouragement, he would soon overcome his inhibitions. Thankfully, with the lewd encouragement of the older men, he finally managed to overcome any reservations he may have had about this act and went for it with gusto! Shoving the nozzle of the funnel unceremoniously into my mouth, he proceeded to let loose a powerful torrent of pee down my throat that kept me swallowing hard to avoid any spillage, which I knew from painful experience was a punishable offence in my master's eyes. The men cheered us on, delighted at this new, amusing way to abuse a slut's mouth and, I'm pleased to say, applauded me at the end as a good 'all-rounder' before taking their own turns to use me as their human piss-pot!

When it was over, and I had guzzled down as much piss as they could produce, Master Matthew suggested the group retire to the lounge for more drinks and, as he humiliatingly put it, "leave the slut to make herself presentable enough to be sent home to her poor hubby". I was left to my own devices in the bathroom to cleanse myself and try and regain some semblance of dignity while, next door, the men discussed me lewdly like a piece of meat.

I waited in the bathroom for more than a hour, until all the men had left. Now that the scenario was over and I was back to being my other 'normal' self, there was no way I wanted to face any of them. I certainly didn't want to see their faces unmasked, anymore than I wanted them to see me. Anonymity was the key to my pleasure.

As I drove home that night, I re-lived the excitement of that memorable evening, going over every delightfully sordid detail. I couldn't wait until my master summoned me for another session. Tomorrow, I would see Matthew at work, but I knew nothing would be said about tonight. His manner would be business-like and detached. And I know there would be moments when I would doubt any of this ever happened. That was the rules of the game that we both knew must be obeyed.

Chapter 7: Pamela

Age: 43, Location: Lincolnshire, United Kingdom

I was introduced to submission and discipline quite unexpectedly in my late thirties. Before then I had never thought about this kind of thing, not even in my fantasies. The way it happened that first time was really a spur of the moment thing and I don't think either of us were prepared for the consequences and the way it would shape our future sex life.

My partner and I had stopped to embrace during a walk through the woods after a picnic. There was some harmless banter between us. Suddenly he pretended to be cross, seized me around the waist and, snatching up my skirt, spanked my bottom sharply several times. This had never happened to me before and although taken unawares, I struggled and wriggled trying to avoid his smacks. Fortunately he was strong enough to hold me and, when it was over, what passion he displayed!

Years later he told me that he had hardly been able to restrain me, which is not surprising given that I am tall and no weakling and certainly far from submissive normally. He said that the struggle was almost too much and he had nearly given up! Thank goodness he didn't, for here was a man at last who could master me!

After that first spanking six years ago, he explained to me the erotic sensation which goes with the discipline scene and I think that I've gradually understood something of the pleasure to be had from what he describes as a form of love making. Whilst I can't claim to enjoy the pain, I do derive satisfaction and, indeed, I am sexually aroused from feeling helpless in my lover's hands. Because I trust him completely not to do me any serious injury I can wallow in his domination, enjoying both his arousal and mine. Subsequent love-making is often intense!

Although he still frequently uses his hand to spank my bottom, and sometimes quite severely too, I have gradually been introduced to a succession of instruments, including a soft leather slipper (which makes more noise than it does damage), a small leather paddle, a tawse, a martinet, a thin flexible cane and, very occasionally, a riding crop—which is by far the worst! Sometimes he makes my punishment a matter of chance. For this a dice is used. Each instrument is allotted a number so that the throw of the dice, which I have to make, decides which one instrument is to be used. Another throw of the dice, added to the first number thrown, indicates the number of strokes. Sometimes I might receive as little as two or as many as twelve. In effect he is making me select my own punishment—which seems to give him an extra thrill!

The presentation of my bottom is always of paramount importance. He doesn't like the skin to be stretched tight so I am never told to touch my toes. Various items of furniture are brought into use. For example, I may have to kneel up on a chair, holding the back or arms, whilst keeping the top half of my bottom jutting out just a little. Alternatively, he might pile enough cushions onto the seat of an easy chair so that when I lay down across both arms my middle is resting on the cushions and my bottom is higher than my feet and head.

Underneath my outerwear he likes me to wear bra, knickers, stockings and suspenders with high heeled shoes. Occasionally, he takes my knickers down himself, which I prefer, but if he is in a mood to humiliate me more than usual, then I am obliged to lower them myself. It is particularly pleasurable to me when he pauses during my punishment to stroke my bottom and to caress me intimately. Always the strokes are administered methodically and slowly. Sometimes he counts; sometimes he makes me count, and a recent refinement was to make me count before the strokes were delivered, so that I was regulating my own punishment. I remember, also, that on one occasion, although he counted the strokes, between each one I had to slowly count a loud "one and two and three and four," up to ten, thus achieving an interval of about ten seconds between delivery. The piquancy of this system meant that I knew exactly when the next stroke would arrive on my smarting bottom.

My experience of being chastised by anyone else occurred when he took me to a lady who "gives lessons". As it was my first (and so far only) visit, she treated me gently and I only received six strokes of the cane over my slip and knickers. He was not present. But, of course, I had to recount for him everything that took place. He still has an erotic fantasy about seeing me beaten by another woman. Strangely enough he has an opposite side to his disciplinary personality which has only revealed itself comparatively recently and which is still developing. He has discovered that he responds to, and is excited by, a lady who is naturally dominant. As yet I haven't witnessed him receiving discipline. But I have seen his bottom afterwards and it is always in a far worse state than mine ever is! The ladies are evidently much more severe with him than he ever is with me! Finally, I have to say how glad I am that "my man" introduced me to this whole new world which is still, I feel, opening out before me.

Chapter 8: Deborah

Age: Unknown, Location: Aberdeen, Scotland

I am a writer. My sexual preference is masochism. I write books about sadomasochism because I enjoy doing it and writing about it, and because my readers enjoy reading about it. I am liberated because I do my own thing, though it paradoxically involves being the opposite of liberated for the duration of the session. Everyone needs a retreat into fantasy, and this safety valve makes a person more competent in the real world and drastically reduces the chances they would translate the fantasy into reality.

Sadomasochists are people (straight, gay or bisexual) who derive sexual satisfaction from the infliction and/or receiving of humiliation and pain. This is probably as good a definition as we will get, but the next question is why? However, I am not about to embark on research that has already been carefully avoided by every psychologist from Freud onwards. The only viable theory is that people are born with such inclinations; our positive reaction is triggered because of some individual connection in our brain.

We did not choose to be this way, but it gives an intensity of pleasure which nothing else can create. The all-important thing is not to feel guilty about it. Lives have been ruined by that artificially induced guilt. If no harm is done, there should be no guilt, and no one is harming anyone (including him or herself) by fantasising over a book or enacting a psychodrama with a willing partner.

It is a scientifically established fact that everyone needs a retreat into fantasy. It makes them better able to cope with reality. Having such an outlet reduces rather than increases the possibility that someone might attempt to translate the fantasy into fact. We are the lucky ones because we acknowledge out interest; many suffer the frustration of being unable to admit, even to themselves, that sado-masochism turns them on.

Real-life SM uses fantasy, but many of my books deal with coercion, abduction, imprisonment, enforced servitude, even if the slave eventually gets to like it. Others show that the slave's desires complement the master's, that both of them are there because they want to be. That is the true to life situation. Those who do not under-stand will see only constraint. Unfortunately, there is the occasional nutter who, we hope, ends up in jail! You do not condemn every one who has sex because there are a few who rape, yet every SM enthu-siast is slandered when a mentally-disturbed person is found to be keeping a woman chained in his basement. We are not dangerous. We are unorthodox, unconventional, doing our own thing (which naturally means we accept that others have an equal right to do their own thing). Of course we are 'different'. I really wouldn't like to be ordinary, would you?

We hear of the criminal who pleads 'pornography drove me to it'. He has been caught. His advisers are seeking to mitigate his sentence. Offer the Establishment a different target (a target they are delighted to attack) and reduce the offenders culpability at the same time. Neither the accusers nor the accused enquire into the validity of the excuse because neither wants its fallacy exposed.

If a person is going to rape or kill, the problem was in his head long before he read a book or saw a video. But some of us take on Society's hang-ups and feel guilty about our own desires. I did not choose to be a masochist; just as other people did not choose to be gay or any other variation from the norm—whatever normal is. Not that it would be 'wrong' if one had decided to be different, but very few people can make a conscious choice about their sexual preferences.

So what causes masochism? There is a theory that inclinations are formed by outside events during early life. In fact, childhood experiences seem to have little relevance. Corporal punishment, for instance, has declined, whilst the number of sadists and masochists have increased, though it may be more accurate to say that the number of sadists and masochists prepared to acknowledge their inclinations has increased.

The only childhood factor which may be relevant in my own case (so it probably applies to many other people) is that my parents never punished me because they did not care what I did. Although I had all the material possessions that I wanted (certainly, enough to arouse the envy of my school friends) I saw that more stable families insisted on certain standards of behaviour and punished transgressions. Perhaps I subconsciously associated punishment with caring. I am aware that I have always had an obsessive need for security, yet this does not explain the sexual arousal caused by humiliation; in most cases this is far more important than pain.

I believe that our enjoyment is triggered in this way because of some individual connections in our brains, some mysterious neurones which make these people called sadomasochists find their delight in the infliction and/or receiving of pain and humiliation. In a sexual context, that is all important.

The orthodox anti-porn campaigners, motivated by religion or politics, have found a common cause with a certain type of feminist who rigidly follows the dogma that pornography represents men exploiting women. Feminists have bound themselves into a straitjacket of their own party line orthodoxy which has become more restrictive than a Victorian whalebone corset. They insist on perpetuating the outdated view of women as victims (I have been called a traitor to my sex because I am a masochist). These feminists are, in effect, attempting to hold back true liberation because an admission that women are no longer oppressed would destroy their raison d'être. Women producing pornography threaten the old-fashioned (but still highly vocal) feminism because female pornographers are more liberated than any feminist could contemplate, or would dare to contemplate!

It has been suggested that feminism is a creed as obsolete as communism or fascism, and no amount of rethinking could breath life into a cadaver. But it still has many supporters, so perhaps we should examine more closely the motivations of its automaton-like fanatics. Although a detailed study is beyond the terms of reference of this article, the one most obvious factor in all life-denying theologies is fear. Fear of the entity or system of belief which they see as the enemy. Feminists fear men. Naturally, they decry this thing which they label pornography because it represents men and women achieving intense pleasure by whatever mode of interaction appeals to them. Another potent factor is envy. Trapped in their own drabness, feminists envy those who have the courage to enjoy life.

Of course, there are commercial interests in all forms of sexual behaviour. There is exploitation. There would be far less of these drawbacks in a free society where sex could be openly acknowledged instead of being forced to operate in the limbo-land of public opportunism and legal restrictions.

Yet there is a more serious objection to sadomasochism. This is the contention that the practitioners of Sado-masochistic sex, especially the dominant member of the partnership, must be of fascist inclination. I thought that the point had been dealt with when it was ascertained that the people who have unusual sexual interests are likely to be of above average intelligence and therefore would not be prone to the 'loser mentality' of fascism. Fascism is an all too obvious classification for someone who likes to inflict pain and humiliation. But in our scene he/she is willing to do it for pleasure and also because the other party derives an intense sexual satisfaction from receiving. Still this accusation keeps recurring.

It is an uncomfortable fact of life that people fantasise about the Nazis. Personally, I do not see how they can be considered dominant, since they created one of the most famous catch phrases of all time: "I was only obeying orders". I do acknowledge the potency of jackboots, though I prefer to think of them as riding boots. This brings us to another type of 'fascist', namely, the Lord of the Manor indulging in his blood sports. Leather is a fetish item, but it is only one of many, and most of those articles or substances bear no unsavoury connotations.

However, fantasies have no resemblance to real life. Whatever props or costumes are used, the participants know that afterwards they are going home to tea, or to the office in the morning. In real life, the Master's power is based solely on the needs and desires of his slaves, though that power is real and can force them to extremes of pain and humiliation, perhaps even more intense because there are no threats, coercion or blackmail. The coercion is in the slave's own natures. The only threat which the Master need ever use is the threat to free a slave. And a successful SM relationship has to contain a greater element of trust than any other form of human association.

Exponents of SM claim that our practices are the most misunderstood of all. Many misconceptions exist, even in the open minds of those libertarians who feel no personal interest in SM and have not studied it. Sadomasochism has nothing to do with standard types, such as the battered wife or hen-pecked husband. Sadomasochism is two or more people choosing to behave in a certain way that gives happiness to all. I emphasise the fact that every participant has chosen to be there. Compulsion, as in the standard fictional scenario of abduction is, to say the least impractical. A more subtle form of compulsion may in some cases exist but it could reasonably be argued that the enthralled one gains more than he or she who loses by the relationship.

The chosen role, whether dominant or submissive, is not necessarily carried over into everyday life. Outside of the sexual scene I am not submissive. Trading in pornographic books in repressive Britain is not for the faint hearted. Yet I cannot get turned onto sex unless a cane or some other instrument of punishment figures in the encounter. Stop asking 'why?'. Just lie back and enjoy it. Or, in my case, bend over and enjoy it!

Yet lives have been ruined by guilt. We feel guilty because society tells us that it is wrong to be different. Our conscious mind recognises the illogic, but the precept is embedded in our subconscious and is therefore dangerous.

Psychologists discovered that people who have unusual sexual interests are likely to be of above average intelligence. So we must be able to deal with our own hang-ups. Submerge the wayward subconscious in logic. The fact that my lover, my master, canes me does not contribute to the ills of the world. In fact, it has the opposite effect. It makes us both happier and so we are better able to do whatever individuals can do to help solve the problems of the world.

Having a good sex life (in whatever mode of expression fulfils one's needs) contributes to the development of a better balanced person. Consider the villains of the past, sublimating their frustration in conquest and genocide. If Hitler had, had a real woman instead of the dim-witted and avaricious Eva, maybe the Holocaust would not have happened. I am not trivialising the worst horror in the blood stained history of the world, but I read somewhere that, at pre-war parties, Hitler always tried to chat up Jewish women, preferring them to the insipid Aryan blondes. One can imagine how those ladies reacted to the insignificant ill-educated man. But looking back and saying 'if only' is an unproductive exercise.

Just as pointless is asking why I want to be hurt and humiliated by the man I love. I can only say it is the greatest thrill and, when I am able to find that fulfilment, I can function optimally in other aspects of life. Sex is important, but it becomes the be-all and end-all of life only when it is frustrated or denied; that is when the trouble starts.

However we must still be secretive. Gays came out, but sadomasochists never attained that illusory acceptance. Regularly, the gutter press 'exposes' so-called 'sick sadomasochists'. We shall never achieve general acceptance because ordinary folk are incapable of understanding refinements of erotica. It is far too good for them. We are the lucky ones because we have found what turns us on, and contentment in that direction sets us free to pursue other aims.

Chapter 9: Lynne

Age: 42, Location: Newport, Wales

I have to always be very careful when talking about this subject because I don't want anyone to get the wrong idea. First and foremost, I am a feminist. This immediately creates a problem in some peoples minds. They think how can she be a feminist and want to be dominated by a man? For a long time I had these problems with myself, so I can understand other feminists recoiling in horror. Before I share my favourite scenarios, let me state my position:

I believe in equality for women in the workplace and in the home. So, when I say that I occasionally enjoy, for instance, being spanked, I want to make several things clear. I'm not being spanked to 'keep me in my place' because my place is equal to everyone else. I am not being 'punished', as I am firmly opposed to corporal punishment for children or for anyone else, for that matter. I'm spanked because I want to be spanked and for no other reason. If I don't want it, I don't get it. It's as simple as that. I'm a free person and I have the right to choose to be spanked or not to be spanked, as my mood dictates. Also, I don't want people using me as evidence that women enjoy being hurt. The vast majority of women, and men, hate being hurt. In the ordinary course of events, so do I. All women are individuals and it's very wrong to tar them with the same brush.

Having said all that, when I'm in a receptive frame of mind and with the right man, of course, I think I could be capable of quite extreme forms of submission. I find it very arousing to be asked in-

timate questions by a dominant man, who wants to find out everything and insists on the truth. I suppose it's a type of humiliation in
itself, having to divulge all one's deepest thoughts, however embarrassing they may be, to a man whose face gives away nothing at all.
As long as I am with a man who can 'read' me and who would know
when 'no' meant exactly that, then I would want to explore and experiment. If the person dominating me has the right approach i.e. a
quiet controlled persuasion rather than shouted rough directions,
then I'm sure I would try almost anything. Or, if the pleasure level is
high then pain becomes equally exquisite.

I had a taste of 'bargaining' with the man who introduced me
to mental restraint. He would tease me with his fingers or mouth
or stand in front of me with his erect cock ready to be sucked and I
would have to 'trade' with him. He would make the bargain slightly
more than I would normally accept. For instance, he would stand
me in the middle of the room with legs spread and hands on head.
He would work me up until I am a begging, quivering mess, slapping
my thighs, buttocks and breasts if I moved or groaned. If I moved
or did make a sound when I wasn't supposed to, he would stop what
he was doing to me and ask, in a very serious tone, if I wanted the
pleasure to proceed. I'm sure you can guess my answer! But I would
have to accept five very painful slaps to each unprotected breast for
the privilege of the continuation of the pleasure.

This next explanation will hopefully let you into my feelings
on 'cock worship'. I love to lie between my partners legs while he lays
relaxed on his back and devour him. It is probably the only way I do
enjoy controlling a man. When his penis is in my mouth I know he is
mine, and I love it! I love to suck and nibble uninterrupted.

But—and it's quite a large 'but'—only after the bargain is struck
and I have paid the price. When I am knelt at his feet awaiting his
instructions and he has tormented me, I must be allowed full rein to
worship the man's cock. I will suck him as he has never been sucked
before. I long to feel the velvet head nudge at my lips and the erect
shaft fill my willing mouth. He will entwine his hands firmly in my
long hair and guide my willing mouth to his cock.

There is such a fine line between what I call 'horny' humili-ation and the other sort. For example, I adore bondage, but in my view, it should be both very secure and very comfortable bondage. I'm sure you realise there are two types of pain. Nothing would per-suade me to accept the wrong sort.

Excuse all my examples, but here's another. If a man decides to fill me so full it brings tears to my eyes, I would enjoy it. But if he is nipping my flesh with a ring at the same time, I would stop him.

I'm not quite sure what I mean by humiliation, but I die of shame if I am forced to expose myself or if I am examined. These acts also blow me away with excitement. My stomach flips at words like 'expose' and 'examine'. I am probably humiliated easier than most people because I am quite dominant at work and in my private life. A partner once made me crawl across the floor on a lead. I rebelled and said 'no way'! I was adamant. But looking back since, I get excited by the thought of being made to, or persuaded to.

I was once a 'coffee table' for an hour. On hands and knees with a sheet of glass on my back. I hated it. But what was suggested by the hands between my legs and the pulling and squeezing of my nipples that hung down exposed made it worth while.

Chapter 10: Karen

Age: 47, Location: London

My 'slave' persona is a very dramatic contrast to how I conduct myself in my normal, every day life. I expect you've heard that a million times before though, haven't you? From what I understand about the mind set of other submissive women they often seem, like me, to come from very respectable backgrounds. My own case is, I'm afraid, resolutely middle class North London Jewish, with all the boring aspects that entails. I work as a teacher part-time in a privileged, private school. I have two lovely children in their early teens and a wonderful husband. It doesn't come more middle class than that, does it? On the surface of it I suppose I have everything a person could want. Yet still I was missing something. Excitement? Adventure? A good, old fashioned zip-less fuck, as Erica Jong would put it? Whatever it was I was ripe for an affair. And, I suppose, when you are in that state of mind you put out, shall we say, certain 'vibes' to the male of the species. I certainly had no lack of offers from male colleges who would have liked an affair with me, but I knew if I was going to have one it would have to be with someone completely un-connected with my life and middle class life style. I wanted a bit of rough, to be perfectly frank with you.

I met my lover, Jeff, who was later to become my master, quite by chance in a pub one lunch time when I was enjoying a drink with some teacher friends. He's a builder by trade and his whole character and working class life style is in stark contrast to my own, which of course is exactly what I was looking for in some extra curricular activity. We've been seeing each other for five years now and I've been his slave for most of that time. To this day, however, he doesn't know my full name or where I live. And that's the way I like to keep it. When we get together it is always through my instigation. Which may be a bit of a contradiction in terms when I am supposed to be the slave. I always phone him and still have the habit of withholding my number, though I know by now to trust him enough not to abuse the situation. Sometimes it can be weeks between meetings. In fact, I only contact when the need becomes unbearable.

In this way the two sides of my life are quite separate, self contained and compartmentalised. There's no chance of an over lap. From the start he fulfilled a part of me that had been denied, perhaps suffocated may be a more appropriate word, in my marriage. Jeff is as coarse and brutal in his manner as my husband, James, is gentle and considerate. While I truly value and appreciate my husband's refined qualities, there has always been a distinct lack of excitement in our lovemaking. Well, on my side anyway. My fantasies have always revolved around being taken and used by some foul mouthed brute and Jeff fits the bill exactly. Unfortunately, or perhaps fortunately, men like that don't come within the sphere of my well ordered world. That's how it started anyway. I had, of course, no idea at the beginning how far it would lead or where this wonderful, frightening journey would take me though, nor the fantastic worlds it would open up for me.

Right from day one of our affair Jeff established his dominance over me. He never asked what I liked in sex, he just took me as his 'right'. My feminist side, which, amazingly enough, I still believed in, would be appalled if someone like my husband had treated me like this, even though it was what I wanted all along. Yet with Jeff it became the most natural and wonderful thing in the world to submit to him as his sex toy. But please don't ask me to explain the contradictions in all this though!

For years I had quietly urged James to try treating me at least a little roughly, but it was always, quite frankly, beyond him. As a combination of new man and old fashioned gentlemen, he simply didn't have it in him. Jeff, by contrast, had it oozing out of every pore in abundance. Whether by instinct or simple disregard for my feelings, he used me in the brutal way I'd always fantasised about.

For instance, he told me on one of my early visits to his house that I was to bring along an extra set of clothes. He didn't even say why, but naturally I did as I was ordered. When I arrived, and without even so much as a warning, he ripped my blouse open and tore apart the clips of my bra. It happened so suddenly that it took my breath right away and made me feel quite faint. But the effect was devastatingly sexy all the same!

This was to become a regular feature of our scenarios. After my clothes were ripped off me or cut away with knives or scissors, I would be forced to stand before him naked while he slapped my breasts back and forth to the rhythm of his abusive and degrading comments, letting me know in no uncertain terms what a vile and dirty bitch I was and all the rest of it.

The sex so far may have been about dominance and abuse, but I hadn't yet been awakened to my full potential for sex slavery. I'll always remember the occasion when, after he'd stripped and slapped my breasts in his usual fashion, he told me he felt it was time to take me to what he called the 'next level down' and asked me if I felt ready. Of course, I hadn't a clue what he was going on about, but that didn't prevent me from saying yes. After all, I'd enjoyed it all so far, so what the hell? Next thing I knew he'd put a leather collar round my neck marked slave and attached a lead to it. I was about to tell him I wasn't too sure about this when he barked an order at me like a sergeant major to get down on my knees. Even I was surprised at how quickly I obeyed. I was then 'walked' around the room like a pet dog and, amazingly, loving every minute of it!

That night when I got back home I found myself lying in bed next to my poor husband re-living the excitement and erotic trauma of that meeting. For days afterwards I couldn't get the thoughts and images of it out of my mind. And it wasn't all pleasant either, I can assure you. In fact, I found the mad pictures going round inside my head quite frightening at times. Thankfully, Master Jeff was experienced enough to help me through this anxious time in my training by telling me this was quite a normal learning curve and was very common in women he had trained in the past as they went through the process of encountering and confronting the demons within themselves.

One demon in particular reared its head time and again and that was the idea of my being used as a whore by any man my master handed me over to. This is something that goes right back to my childhood, to a time before I even knew the word or what it meant. I do remember vividly the power and excitement and the value it put upon myself to make the boys in my neighbourhood hand over their pocket money to see me lift my skirt and my knickers for them. Later, as I grew up, I would be guaranteed to get really turned on asking a boyfriend if he would pay to have sex with me and how much he would be prepared to spend. I know a lot of women would find this idea totally repugnant and demeaning, but to me, despite my being a feminist, the idea of being a prostitute had always brought with it a certain sense of importance and self worth. If a guy is willing to pay for it, then a girl must be worth it!

The whore bit carried on through college where I was often 'helped, shall we say, financially by a few well heeled older married gentlemen in return for certain favours of a sexual nature. Obviously, I discussed all this with my master and he decided it was splendid subject matter to incorporate into our games.

I remember the first time was with a mini cab driver who took me over to Jeff's house one night. Jeff always insisted on paying for my cab as this involved him handing over money at the end of the session while I was still dressing, just like a real prostitute being paid for her services. Anyway, I admitted to Jeff that I found the young driver very sexy and, in fact, I had already booked him from my journey home later that night.

My attraction to the young man became the centre point of our games that night, culminating in Jeff's command that I should seduce him on the return trip. He went on to tell me exactly how I was to accomplish this, too! He said I should begin by bringing up the subject of how lots of girls, especially young and drunk ones on a Saturday night, would try to get out of paying their fares by offering some form of sex to the cab drivers. Usually a blow job or hand relief. I must confess the scenario both thrilled and scared the hell out of me, but by the time I was ready to leave I was well into the idea. As I tried to get dressed, Master Jeff stopped me and demanded to know what the hell I was doing putting my bra and panties back on as he said real whores like me never wear undies. He immediately confiscated them into my handbag. He then proceeded to make me look more 'presentable' as a whore. This entailed forcing me to leave the top three buttons of my blouse undone so the driver could get a good look at my boobs.

When it came time for my departure for home and the cab was waiting outside, Jeff did something he'd never done before. He walked me outside and right up to the taxi and handed me my money in full view of the driver, calling it my 'wages' for the evening. If that wasn't embarrassing enough, he then turned me round to face him with my back to the cab and, while he kissed me goodnight, he inched up my short skirt to give my driver a good eyeful of my bare bottom. As you can imagine, my master took great delight in whispering into my ear that the guy couldn't take his eyes off my rear.

For the first few minutes of the drive home I was completely flustered with a mixture of excitement and embarrassment. I'm only glad it was dark so the driver couldn't see my crimson cheeks!

Such was the power that Jeff held over me by this stage of the game that I felt there was no way I could get out of the challenge he had set me. It was as if he was somehow in the vehicle with us watching every move. He had told me to phone him from my mobile the minute I was dropped off and before I went into the house where, hopefully, my hubby would be fast asleep by now, to inform him what had happened. As I'm such a bad liar anyway, he would know if I was concocting a story. I know it sounds crazy but I felt I had no choice but to go through with it, even if it meant forcing myself on the poor young man who, you have to understand, was young enough to be my son!

I suppose you want me to go into all the sordid details about what happened that night, don't you? Well, I followed my master's instructions and got the conversation round to asking him about any sexy interludes he might have experienced in his job. It turned out he did indeed have quite a few juicy anecdotes to tell. Apparently, drivers get propositioned on a regular basis by young girls. But not, it would seem, by women my age. After I'd managed to steer the conversation round to the subject of sex, it was only a small step to actually doing it. In fact, the act took place in a secluded side street not far from where I live. No, I won't go into the details. Sex is just sex. What was important here was the control my master had in making me do it even when he wasn't there!

After that incident with the cab driver Master Jeff decided to turn me into his whore. I had no objection this at all, as it had always been a fantasy of mine anyway. I've always loved that French film 'Belle du Jour' with Catherine Deneuve. You know, the one where she is this respectable suburban house wife who works in a brothel in the afternoon, just for kicks.

My new whore name was to be Sophie as Master felt I would be able to separate the two sides of my personality off much easier that way. There would be no over lapping of my normal self and my whore self. I could, in effect, put Sophie on and off take a coat. I expect that is the way real prostitutes do it. Naturally, Jeff appointed himself as my pimp!

One way Jeff got me into 'whore-mode' was to take me into Central London and around the West End to places where street walkers operate. He'd stay in the car or position himself on the other side of the road so he could still keep an eye on me but, at the same time, not frighten off potential 'clients'. You must understand though, I never actually went off with any of the men who approached me. That wasn't in the rules of Jeff's game and was obviously far too dangerous. No, I was just after the thrill of being looked over by the men, maybe occasionally talking to them about what they were after, but generally simply getting to the idea of thinking and behaving like a prostitute. Which I did really well, I think! I used to love watching the real prostitutes at work, and copied the way they stood and walked over to the cars to talk to men. I found that wonderfully, erotically seedy!

However, after playing with that scenario for a while, the thrill did begin to wear a bit thin for both of us, and we both knew it was now time to move onto the next stage, which was to do it for real! To ensure my absolute safety, Master Jeff only allowed me to play whore with men he knew personally and trusted. These were all friends of his from the fetish and swinger scenes.

One other thing my master tuned into with me psychologically was my attitude to black men. He considered this to be the final taboo, the final barrier, if you will, toward my becoming a complete slut-slave. Basically, to understand this, you need to understand where I am coming from culturally. I was born and raised in Cape Town, South Africa and grew up in, admittedly, a very privileged position. We had servants and house boys, gardeners and all the rest of it. Now, I'm not racist at all, far from it. I mean, I actually campaigned against apartheid as a student and got myself into a lot of trouble with the authorities because of it. In fact, that's one of the reasons I eventually left and came to live in this country.

But you must understand how it affects you when you live in a place like that. No matter what your personal feelings about the race issue, you simply can't get away from the deep rooted regard of black people as little more than animals. It is something I hated in myself and still do. But it's right in there in the national psyche and there's no way anyone in that country can get away from it. It's as simple and as fundamental as that.

When my master became aware of this side of me, he decided to use it as a tool in my degradation. The idea of me being fucked by black men would come up time and time again during sex play. He knew, of course, that I was at my most vulnerable then and my imagination was at its most susceptible to any kind of scenario, no matter how bizarre or revolting.

There were many ways he set out to achieve, what you might

term, sexual 'brain washing'. Sometimes he would incorporate it with our usual whore fantasies, or I wouldn't get his cock or a present until I admitted that I secretly wanted to fuck a black man. Other times, he would pose the most outrageous questions. For instance, given the choice would I rather eat shit or fuck a black man. Once I'd admitted that, obviously, between the two I'd rather go with a black man, it gave him a doorway to open into my mind with which he could further humiliate me. His most favourite method, and the one that got to me the most, was when he introduced the fantasy character of 'Julius' into our bedroom games. For this, he'd tie me to the bed and blindfold me and tell me he was leaving the room but that Julius would be here shortly to fuck the ass off me. He'd leave me alone for five, sometimes ten minutes, sometimes longer. During which time I would be tortured with anticipation and become very aroused, yet feel very degraded at the same time.

The character of Julius was played by my master, of course. He was a very big, very powerful and very brutal black man who loved to use white women. Especially, as he put it, stuck up, white bitches like me. By the time I heard Julius come into the bedroom, I'd be in an incredibly excited state. My master, talking in a rather good impression of a West Indian accent, would launch into a sneering tirade of all the things he was going to do with his big black cock to a white cunt like me. He'd maintain the most filthy sex banter while he was abusing me. Knowing exactly what I liked to hear in bed, I'd become almost deranged with excitement.

Gradually, through the weeks and months of this sexual brainwashing, my sexual arousal and thoughts of black men would become intertwined to the point where I wasn't quite sure anymore where my desires truly lay. Were they his fantasies I was responding to or were they mine all along? It seemed some door had really been opened by master into my psyche. Perhaps I had really been in a state of denial all these years about my attraction to black men? As yet he hasn't actually set me up with any black guys, but I'm sure that treat will come. And, with my master's help and guidance, I'm sure I will be ready for it.

Chapter 11: Nicola

Age: 23, Location: London

I am fairly new to the scene and, because I am strong willed, I've always felt I needed to be trained to learn to respect a master and how best to please a man. I've no interest in anal sex or drinking urine or anything like that, but I am very keen to experiment with discipline beginning with a protracted course of postal training. What I would hope to gain from my training would be a total understanding of how to worship a man's body. I have always found that I am hindered in my ability to 'let go' by worrying that I have not learnt the most I can to worship and satisfy the male and therefore I find I can't create the erotic situations I crave.

I've never yet found any man who is willing to teach me in the art of satisfying him and this adds to my frustration. I don't want to keep having 'unopen', deadened relationships. I am turned on by the idea of being trained and disciplined by a 'master'; someone who can teach me body worship. This way I can relinquish control and release myself to pure feeling. I am excited by the idea of being used as an animal, unhindered by paranoia, purely trained to worship and serve. I have spent much of my life 'in my head' and not my body. Hopefully, in a safe situation, I will be able to truly feel and to connect with my master on a totally open and sensual level.

I would hope for a strong mental relationship as well as the physical side, for I feel it is the same. One affects the other and both are equally important. I would wish to be silent, unless otherwise directed; for, again, I desire the release of mental control. I would wish to learn of my power as a woman through total acknowledgement of my energy and qualities and not through female false words and worry.

I am just starting to study massage and I would like to use oils and tactile situations in a subtle way, as well as a more blatant way. For example, using light touch and scented oils to worship my master's body as well as times of being whipped. I want to explore all areas of eroticism from mental to the physical senses.

I realise that my answers are fairly broad, but basically I would like to learn to serve a man in all the ways he chooses. He may lick and tease my body or he may lightly whip my backside. His touch alone is sufficient. I would be merely thankful he is touching me and making my body throb for him.

This is one of my favourite scenarios which, I'm pleased to say I have pretty accurately created in real life. My Master and I go out to dinner in a smart restaurant. We meet at the reception desk. It is a hotel type country residency. I am wearing an elegant suit with a silk blouse with my hair up, make up and ear-rings. I can feel my nipples free against the silk. I wear no underwear, only a chastity belt. The belt is tight, pulling up hard against my cunt. I can feel my sex throbbing under the smart suit. I wear highish heels and appear as an independent, attractive, fairly rich young woman.

The Master is also dressed smartly. He carries a red silk scarf in his pocket, which I know he will use to gag me with if I speak out of turn.

Once we meet in the foyer I hand over the key to the belt. In an unspoken agreement I am his for the night. Beyond this point I am under his control. Until I get the key back I am his to train as an animal in the arts of eroticism and serving. I am not to speak my mind unless specifically asked. I am to watch my answers and words at all times. I must not appear to have any other life apart from serving. If I do speak I know that later I shall be gagged and criticised and insulted for daring to think I have the right to exist independently. I am told I am ugly and deserve no attention from the Master. No touch, no spankings. Only the gag and harsh words telling me of my unworthiness. At worst I will be tied up and watched by the Master critically for a long time. I am denied the Masters touch, which is all my life exists for. To serve and be rewarded. Punishment ultimately lies in total lack of emotional feedback. I have ceased to exist in my Master's eyes. I can be left there for an hour or so to think on my mistakes and my crimes in assuming I am important enough to stop serving the Master.

If the master wishes to torture me he may tie my hands to a bed or chair or even a pair of stocks. He then covers my eyes with a blindfold and walks around my body without touching me. I can feel his presence. It makes me wet, but I have not served him well enough to be rewarded with touch.

When he does touch me he sometimes investigates my body as if I were some animal at a market. I am forced to suffer the humiliation of not knowing if I am good enough to be of use to him.

At the restaurant I am the embodiment of a perfect paid mistress or kept wife. I laugh at the right times and make sure I do not get overexcited and unladylike. I must look only at the Master for I know he will punish me for daring to see others. I am his alone.

My throbbing gets deeper as we eat and he tells me in a low voice what he will do to me later if I have behaved. The food is used to show me how base I am and that all is sexual. All are fluids and flesh and that I must never think myself more than this, for then I may not serve the Master.

The meal is spent without touch, only words. A string of crudities and eroticism building up to make my desire complete. I feel my sex getting damp and hot beneath my chastity belt.

We leave and he drives me to his house. He still does not touch me. He reminds me that in my smart clothes and independent look I am merely satisfying his whim to show others his magnificence.

We arrive at the house and I must leave the car and open his door. He climbs out and fastens a collar around my neck and leads me into his world.

Once inside I remove my skirt and have to follow him on all

fours wherever he goes. He spends an hour doing normal things while I must follow and obey his desires. He sits and instructs me to come and sniff his crotch and beg for him like a bitch on heat, licking and pawing him. He may be fairly rough with me, though he does not want to hurt me. But I must be taught my place.

My Master makes me lie on my back on the carpet with my legs spread wide and my sex vulnerably exposed. He has tied the lead to a chair and now he inspects me to see if I was a worthy buy. He insults me a little yet adds odd phrases of appreciation to let me know what rewards I will be allowed if I behave. The greatest of all rewards is to be allowed to lick his body clean and sniff at his beautiful balls.

Next my Master removes his trousers to let me get hopeful. He allows me to sit up and smell him and to lick greedily at his cock and balls. But he only does this to get me excited and tease me cruelly. Suddenly he steps back just beyond reach to where my hungry mouth cannot get at him. All I can do is look up and adore my god.

Sometimes I am allowed to take oils to massage and suck my Master's feet. But I must avert my eyes at all times from his sacred sex, hovering erect and magnificent above me. All the while I attend to him I know he is watching me closely, waiting to insult and punish me if I displease him.

Finally he rewards me by tying me bent over a chair or bed. Then he starts to spank me, gently building up the power of his blows. By this time my cunt is flowing and all I desire is him and his attention.

If I have pleased him he will blindfold me and do as he wants with my body. He may lick and tease me or he may lightly whip my backside, running the tip down the edge of the chastity belt. His touch alone is sufficient to make me fly.

I am merely to be thankful he is paying me attention and making my body throb for him.

He will then take off the blindfold and, standing over me, order me to kiss and tongue his penis. He teaches me how to please him well. If I do not learn as well as I should he removes himself and spanks me again. I am reminded that I am only here to learn the arts of pleasing him and that I have no other purpose. He teaches me to use my tongue and hand well. At first I am clumsy, but I am only young and he allows me some leeway to learn.

Once he has come in my mouth he will chain me to the wall and let me think on how well I have just performed my act of worship. If I have pleased him he will release me and drink my juices which are, of course, his and made only for him. If I am not good then I must remain where I am.

It is his choice whether I leave still in the belt and take the key (which marks the end of our meeting and his ownership) or whether he thinks I have learned well enough to be allowed to stay longer in his presence.

If I have been good he will release me and make me walk on all fours like an animal with lead and collar. He takes me around the house. He may even decide to honour me by masturbating onto my face and breasts and leaving me to enjoy the feeling of his essence drying on my bound body.

There is an exciting uncertainty. He may tie me up and leave me or he may occasionally spray me with urine to mark me off as his territory if I have looked at other men thoughtfully. This act will be done with him fully dressed and me naked and tied. At this point I must look into his eyes at all times to show my devotion while I am anointed.

If I am really good he may decide to enter me in which ever way he chooses.

My best way is to be tied to a whipping cross and fucked straight on. But any way is total joy at being honoured.

At all times the Master is the Lord I serve and obey. The One who has agreed to teach me the many ways to please a man.

I have a secret word to stop the proceedings if I get too scared. At this point the key is returned and I must leave without another word. I then reflect on all that has passed before I next see the Master and hand over my key once more.

Chapter 12: Sabrina

Age: Unknown, Location: United Kingdom

I suppose I was born submissive and couldn't have been anything else, even if I'd wanted to be. My first real experience of being dominated was when the three brothers who lived next door took me down to the shed at the bottom of the garden and ordered me to pull down my knickers. They were younger than me, but I knew they meant business. I did as I was told, and felt as though I was nothing just standing there with my pants around my ankles and my dress hitched up over my chest, while they stood there giggling.

The eldest wanted to rub his dick up and down my pussy. I stood there while the other two laughed, taking the mickey out of me while their brother spat his cream over my stomach. He then told me he'd finished with me for now and that I should pull up my pants.

It was obvious that the others had got the message; before too long his cousin was in on the act. We only lived in a small country village so there were plenty of secluded places for them to 'train' me. Soon I was servicing practically every male in their family! Though nothing as yet had entailed intercourse, my vagina being still unexplored territory, I'm afraid the same couldn't be said for the rest of me! My tits and arse and especially my mouth were all used to the full. They told me often enough that my mouth was for fucking, not talking!

Then I moved house, somewhere less remote, and here I met Chris. He was my first real master, who taught me to do as I was told and not ask questions. His brother was also his slave, but I was to be his total sex slave. He even made his brother watch, through the window from outside in the pouring rain, while he entered my vagina for the first time. But it was never with his cock. I desperately wanted to feel his cock really deep inside me, but he wouldn't do it. He told me that, as this was my first lesson, I'd have to earn the rest. Slaves, apparently, only got his fingers!

If I did something wrong, or didn't appear eager enough for his attentions, he would drag me by my hair into his bedroom and tie my hands to the headboard. The pain was part of the pleasure and my body would invariably heighten with anticipation. Each time I hoped this would be it. He'd suck and bite on my nipples and thrust his cock into my mouth, ramming it so hard I'd almost gag on it. Then he'd come whenever he desired. Sometimes my hair and face would be caked in his sperm by the time he'd finished with me. He'd then usually force my legs as wide apart as they would go so that his slave-brother could give my pussy and sperm smeared face a good licking. He used to like to make his younger brother swallow his sperm, which I remember really shocked me at first. But then a slave gets used to anything, doesn't she? It wouldn't have done for me to make a mess of my master's bed because part of our slave duties was to ensure that his rooms were kept spotless. Our relationship ended when he found another slave girl who he preferred to me.

My next master saw me getting off a bus one day and decided I was to be his. He had many slaves, yet he was willing to give me the honour of being his Number One Slave. Again my duties were mainly of a sexual nature, but I was also to provide meals for him and his guests on demand. Master Dick always entertained at least once a week. Like any slave, I was nothing, simply there to do as was bidden. He really enjoyed passing me around to be used by his male friends and guests, telling me how badly I had performed and punishing me for it in front of them. This was the second part of my slave training. He was much more strict than Master Chris had been, having a cruel tongue on him he had no need of whips. Master Dick would cut through anyone, especially me, with a cutting remark.

I had to be at his beck and call at all times. Quite often in the middle of the night I would be shaken awake to provide sexual relief for my master, or any of his guests. As he entered me, he loved to chant over and over: "You are mine. You are mine". Then he would insist that I chanted back something like: "I am yours. I am yours." If I was good and obeyed I would be allowed to go back to sleep after an hour or so of his abuse. If not, he would make sure I got no sleep at all and was kept tormented all night long. Incidentally, Master Dick has given me his permission to reveal that this is no joke name for he was christened Richard.

I have another master now, after ten years with my previous owner, who I provided with two children during our time together. Obviously, they still live with him, Just as he regarded my cunt as his property, so he regards my children as his property too. My two daughters are cared for by his subsequent Number One Slaves, but I am given permission to see them at specified times. Master Dick's present slave recently bore him another child, whom the elder two look after while she sees to his every need. Incidentally, I should mention that I am forbidden to mention the Number One Slave in between, as she disobeyed him and was subsequently punished and is no longer to be spoken of. She, I believe, is now aiming to become a mistress!

I must say that I am very happy serving my present master. Master A (he doesn't want his name mentioned here) knows I am well trained as a sex slave. He too has other slaves, but they are much lesser in status than I. He even permits me to indulge in their subjugation, but only so far. Naturally, I must always follow what he says and never do or say anything that would interfere with his desires. This pleases me for I know my boundaries.

I have had to learn his moods and ways. In the beginning it was purely guess work and I made a few mistakes, for which I was duly punished. He gets black moods when nothing I can do is right; then I try to get on with my duties without having to speak to him, or have as little contact as possible.

Then one day he decided I was to be slave to both him and another woman. She was not one of his slaves, however, but a mistress. I knew it was going to be one of his games, he likes playing games! Her name was Selena and, having met her once previously, I was a bit wary. She was part Spanish and could have a bit of a temper if provoked. Yet it also stimulated a spark of anticipation in me that my master could sense. Fortunately this pleased him. Mistress Selena then took over control of me, informing me that I was to be her sex-slave, as well as his, for the night.

Even after all these years I had never been with another woman, remarkably none of my previous masters had ever ordered it. There was then a little apprehension, intermingled with a quite unexpected tingle between my legs at the prospect of it though. She seemed to sense this and appeared to became a little annoyed by my presumption. I knew this was not a good beginning, for if the mistress was not pleased then neither would my master be!

Without further ado, she ordered me to strip for punishment. As always, I did what I was told. I bent over as directed, but I didn't enjoy the first sensation of her hand as it came in contact with my bum. After the first few slaps there was a feeling of warmth that belied the severity of each motion. I knew that this was necessary, for a slave is supposed to welcome a superior to themselves; to succumb unconsciously, which I had not done. Luckily my master intervened at this point, telling her to show a little tolerance as it was my first time being used by a woman. I was so grateful to him for this reprieve. Of course it meant a service would be required later, but I could do that only as long as my arse wasn't too sore!

I had heard that mistresses quite often had another who dominated them, but up until now I had never seen it with my own eyes. For she did as he requested and the anger on her face subdued, to my intense relief! As time passed I began to wonder who was the more dominant of the two. It struck me that mistresses were more severe than a lot of masters to their sex-slaves. Though I had to admit I admired her, not only for her fiery ways, which were initially intimidating, but also for her beautiful body. Mistress Selena had an adorable physique, all soft and subtle. Her skin was so flawless and so smooth to the touch.

The first time she ordered me to caress and satisfy her demands I felt as though I was in heaven. Closing my eyes I let my fingers glide around her every curve. She allowed me that pleasure, not because she knew I enjoyed it, but because she didn't want me to look at her body. She forbade me and, eventually, even had my eyes bandaged to make sure I couldn't feast my eyes on her nakedness. But that didn't stop me from imagining as I played with her nipples, ran my tongue down her stomach, then lapped up her juices. I had to make sure she was spotless down there before she left. Some evenings it would take literally hours before I achieved this goal! The process could go on for even longer when my master decided to join in. Most of the time he just enjoyed watching the two of us, but sometimes he would take part, usually fucking me from behind as I pleasured my mistress.

I must say, she wasn't as easy to please as all that! It was quite common for her to grasp my nipples and pinch them quite viciously if I wasn't going as hard as I should. One of her favourite pastimes was to spread eagle me to the bed and for both of them to use me together to get their pleasure. Mistress Selena would often bring her various 'toys' with her. They would try out each one on me and then give them grades as to how good they were or whether they were of any use, or even how many to use at one time! I'm afraid I'm forbidden to reveal any details regarding these 'toys'. Mistress Selena is very strict about her privacy. In fact, I feel I dare not say anymore really. I'm sorry.

Chapter 13: Evie

Age: 60, Location: New Hampshire, USA

My ten year old self never wants to be spanked. Daddy, however, spanks me about five times a day, which is nowhere near enough for my sixty year old self!

The above was written by my sixty year old self, of course. Now my ten year old self speaks her mind. I don't want or need to be spanked, ever! Daddy insists that my behaviour is better if I get the usual five spankings. He feels I need more than that, but, every time he really gives me all that I need, his shoulder hurts for the next two days. He wants your help in disciplining me. Now I wouldn't mind if you came over and just played games with me. I would mind a lot if you felt you had to help Daddy with my discipline. Look at this way. All those spankings aren't working, so how about not doing them? Spanking is a pretty childish way to discipline a ten year old anyway. Now that I am starting to develop into a young woman, it is awfully humiliating to have to expose myself to everyone who decides that I need to be spanked. Last time we visited the "Hellfire Club" in New York City, it seemed a lot of the men there felt that I had to be spanked. I could hardly sit the next day. Now, I think I am a perfectly nice little girl who behaves just fine. If I should goof up, just let me know with your voice, not your hand, please! I never want to get spanked, nor do I ever need to be spanked. I wish I could make everyone aware of this!

I thought that I would give you some of my experiences and

preferences. Maybe I will give you some of my fantasies, too. When I was very young, I had a kind of floating, nebulous interest. I wasn't quite sure why I enjoyed certain cartoons more than others. That interest crystallised when I was ten years old. The first spanking I ever received was given to me by my father. It was the only one he ever gave me. My mother didn't spank me at all. As I say, I was ten at the time.

He had just come home from work where he was a foreman of carpenters. He had heavy calluses on his hands from all the hammers and saws. There were no electrical tools then. He was physically tired. He was sitting in his easy chair reading the paper. TV was invented, but not in very many homes yet. My mother was putting the finishing touches on dinner. I wanted attention. I crawled up into my father's lap between his stomach and his newspaper. He grabbed my ankles as he stood up. He placed my ankles on his left shoulder and held them in place with his left arm. I was hanging upside down, down his front side. With his right hand, he spanked me a number of times on my slacks covered bottom. I wasn't counting the spanks, but I was hanging for quite a while. Maybe I received ten or fifteen spanks, I really don't know. I know I cried more from fear than from the pain because he had never touched any of us girls before. Finally, he turned me back right side up, sat back down and picked up his evening paper again. It hurt for over an hour, certainly throughout dinner that was called soon after.

Another important event happened when I was ten. I saw a boy get spanked at school. It was while I was in fifth grade. We were doing some sort of seat work. The teacher was talking quietly to a boy on the far side of the room. Then she did something I'd never seen a teacher do before. She left the classroom and returned, a couple of minutes later with the male principle. He was carrying a wooden paddle, a little larger than a Ping-Pong bat and half an inch thick. The teacher called this boy to the front of the class. She told him to assume the position. I still remember how he looked up at her and said, "I don't understand" with a very scared expression on his face. The female teacher demonstrated what she meant by placing her hands on a chair seat, bending over and keeping her legs straight. The boy assumed the position. The principal went behind him and swung the paddle way back and then forward, hitting him as hard as he could on his jeans covered bottom. He swung back again and gave him another swat. He then told the boy to return to his seat. As the boy turned around, we could see tears streaming down his face. He told us that it hurt. Probably the tears were more from embarrassment than pain. The principal left and the teacher taught a very quiet class for the rest of the day.

After that, I knew what I wanted. When I was twenty, I met my first husband. I told him of my interest. He thought I should be committed to a mental institution. Obviously, I wasn't going to get any understanding from him. After twenty three years, we divorced for reasons that had nothing to do with my interest in getting spanked. Another twelve years, I got up the courage to enter an adult bookstore. Not many females frequent those shops. I found a few magazines. They were not exactly what I wanted, but they had advertisements for better magazines. I sent off for a few of these better ones. One of the magazines I sent for was Stand Corrected put out by Shadow Lane in Los Angeles. I wrote to some of the men who advertised there.

My first adult spanking occurred from answering one of these ads. We wrote back and forth and talked on the phone before meeting. I stressed that I didn't want any sex to occur at all. He agreed to that stipulation or, at least, I thought he did! We met at a restaurant and then adjourned to his hotel room where he gave me three hundred smacks with his hand. It left me with huge bruises all over my bottom. He asked if it was a good spanking. I assured him it was. He then spoiled it by saying that he wanted sex in return for such a good spanking! I said, "Nothing doing". He walked me to my car and asked again. Again I said no. He called a week later and then again a month later and asked if I would reconsider and get a spanking in exchange for sex. Again I said no. I never heard from him again.

My next spanking was audio taped. I went with another girl so I wouldn't have the problem of sex coming up. We were both spanked by this man she knew. I was supposed to be ten and she was eight. The man in question had spanked her before, so he started off the session with her while I watched. Then he alternated between us. We both received excellent spankings. I have the audio tape still to prove it! My next spanking was video taped up in Washington State. My ex and the man's girl friend were there watching. I've got the video tape, too.

I've had so many experiences since I found my true self within the spanking community. My daughters, who are both full grown, know all about my interest, though they don't understand it. My eldest daughter is studying to be a journalist. It is her dearest wish to write the religious page for a newspaper. My son doesn't have the slightest idea. Now that I have greater knowledge and experience, and knowing now that there are some dangers with this sport as with many other sports, I have come up with a list of preferences. I have good reasons for many of these, but they are only preferences; they are not written in stone!

I prefer leather implements like your hand, leather paddles, straps, tawse, belt, riding crop and razor strop. I don't like wood such as a hairbrush, oven shovel or cane. I prefer leather because I have found I can take more spanks with leather than I can with wood, so the spanking can last longer. Wood is also very hard on the skin.

I prefer my bottom supported over something, such as your knee, a table or a bed. I don't like to have to touch toes, or knee to chest positions on a bed. My favourite position is with you seated on a bed or sofa, me over your left knee with your right leg holding my legs, my knees near the floor and my torso on the bed or sofa. It is a comfortable position for both of us, so the spanking can last a long time.

I like light bondage, such as my wrists bound in front with nylon Velcro handcuffs while over the knee, or even in bed at night so I can't rub myself. Another time would be while I am bent over a table with my hands secured to the other end and my ankles in a spreader bar. I have found that bondage increases my pleasure about double. I don't like my thighs spanked, but do feel it has a place. If I yell too loudly or move too much, a word from you and a few spanks to the thigh will quiet me down.

The next thing is something you may not want to do and can easily be skipped, if you would prefer. I am curious to know if the temperature of my bottom increases during a spanking. If a thermometer could be inserted in my arse just before and again after, my curiosity could be satisfied. Instead of using Vaseline as a lubricant, try Metholatum. It burns a little so is more effective. Vic's Vapour Rub burns too much. I have a butt plug, too. It could be inserted before the spanking and will remain in during the spanking. I also have a rectal dildo. If it was inserted after a spanking and before corner time, it will stay in while my legs are together. It gets interesting if you then require me to separate my legs a few inches and then a few inches more. When the dildo falls out, it is time for more spanking.

I love being lectured and don't mind corner time if accompanied by a lecture. I don't like corner time if left all by myself. I prefer to be spanked in a warm place because then I can take more spanks than when punished in a cold place. The woodshed in winter is not a warm place! I would also appreciate it if you would rub my bottom during a spanking, because then I can take two or three times the number of spanks than if you don't. A hug afterwards is nice too!

I like to be spanked rather hard. Twelve men so far have told me that they never spanked anyone harder than they have spanked me! I prefer not to get bruises and don't want cuts or blisters. I sometimes cry during a spanking. If I should cry when you are spanking me, I would like you to glance at the clock and note the time. Continue whatever you were doing that brought on the tears for five full minutes. You see, when I really break down and start crying, I have become truly ten years old again! I can't use a safe word, but it won't hurt me to cry for five minutes. Once the five minutes are over, slow up and lighten up and bring the spanking to a halt. Mainly I love to spanked and want it to last a very long time! I don't think four hours of spanking at a time is excessive, do you? I also love to be spanked by very tall men because it makes my fantasy of being only ten years old more real. Even standing, I have to look up as I did when I was ten.

I would just like to say, at this point, that I am very glad that you are where you are and not here. I am afraid that if you ever came here, I'd end up with my end up!

This brings me onto my fantasies, some of which I have lived out. Some are impossible to live out. And some I would very much like to live! Here's my school fantasy.

After the school bus has left, you find me still in bed. I tell you that I'm sick. You put me over your knee to check the temperature in my rectum. After three minutes, it is obvious that I'm not sick at all. As I'm already in position, you decide a hand spanking is called for. Then you order me to get breakfast.

After breakfast, I wash the dishes with maybe a few helpful swats from you. You take me to school from the kitchen to the dining room. That is the principal's office. He puts me either over the desk or the back of our couch and straps me.

I finally get to class. An oral geography test is going on. The text is the World Almanac. The teacher gives a state name, and I have to come up with its capital. I actually had to learn all the state capitols in 'real' fifth grade, but have since forgotten them. By the way, Daddy is still very upset that I can't name them all, nor can I list all the states in fifteen minutes, which is what we fifth graders are supposed to do. I also hate long division, and think that calculators were invented to eliminate long division. How can I stress it more? Oh, I forgot to mention that the class is held in our bedroom. Anyway, when I miss a capitol, I get spanked in front of the whole class (that is, in front of Daddy or in front of you). After a number of misses and spankings, it is obvious I didn't study. My teacher takes me to the principal to be spanked once more.

Back at class, and now a spelling test is going on. The text is a dictionary. The teacher gives me a word and I have to spell it. When I misspell a word, he spanks me once for each letter as he spells it correctly. Then he spanks me once for each letter as I spell it correctly five times. After a number of words and spankings, it becomes obvious that I didn't study at all. He again sends me to the principal for further discipline.

Returning to class, I plot revenge. I see my chance and throw a well-chalked blackboard eraser at my teacher. It hits right on the rump of his navy blue trousers. The other kids laugh. I am proud of my aim. The teacher grabs me and spanks me hard. It seems there is some silly rule about not assaulting a teacher! He sends me again to the principal, who ties me over the back of the couch and whips me soundly. Then he does something I wish he didn't do. He sends a note home. I know that means my uncle will use his razor strop and send me to bed without dinner.

My Junior (for kids) Army fantasy: I am a private in a junior army, and a sergeant is drilling me. My skirt is pinned up and my panties removed, displaying my bare bottom for all to see. When I make a mistake in drill, he hits me hard with a riding crop as a signal to bend over for more.

Chapter 14: Snowball

Age: 30, Location: United Kingdom

Firstly, I can tell you I'm thirty and female. My pony name is Snowball because my coat is very pale. I'm at present in a permanent relationship with a Mistress. She currently has one other slave who isn't really into the pony scene. I've been actively involved in the BDSM scene for about four years and wish I'd had the courage to try it when I was younger.

One of the reasons I fell for my partner originally was that she knew about the pony scene. The idea of being a pony girl had fascinated me for years, but I'd never had the opportunity or courage to try it. It appeared to me to be an excellent way to serve a Master or a Mistress, to pull them along in a carriage. Being fairly fit, I hoped I'd be able to cope. Also, the dependency, humiliation and lack of human responsibilities that come with the animal role play appealed to me very much. The first time we tried it was magical. Once Mistress took my bit out, she couldn't shut me up for days. It was as good as I'd dreamt it might be.

When I'm a pony, I can relax and stop thinking about all the distractions that come with being a human. I have no responsibilities except to do what I'm told, it's a wonderful way to relax. In most other submissive roles, you have to do at least some thinking for yourself, but in pony role you can become utterly passive. Being driven with a bit in your mouth is wonderful because the instructions from your rider are silent. With training, all the commands from your Master or Mistress can become nonverbal.

Other uncommon aspects of pony play in comparison to other forms of sub/dom scenarios are that it takes place outdoors. Being practically naked can be wonderful in the sunshine, or invigorating in the winter frosts, and all that running around pulling carts helps keep you fit as well. While the bondage can be quite severe, the idea is that you can still run.

I enjoy many other submissive and power exchange roles, ranging from my normal 24/7 servitude to my Mistresses' needs, through to fairly intense bondage and corporal punishment scenes. We also enjoy other role play scenes such as school, maid service and prostitute games. I should add that, being bisexual, it isn't a problem for me to serve either Masters or Mistresses. What real pony has that choice anyway? They can be male or female, gay or straight, large or small. It's more important to me that they want to, and don't feel the need to ask me, for instance, if it's okay to gallop or go round the track again. If that's what they want to do, then they should just do it.

Pony training takes many forms, from dressage on the end of a long rein, blindfold driving (which, I'm afraid, I'm not very good at), to general fitness training. At first I found it quite hard to wear a bit and have my arms bound behind me for long periods of time, but now I can cope almost all day and my elbows will even touch behind my back.

Punishment is usually administered using a short crop or medium length dressage whip, both sharp and cutting in feel. Encouragement using the whip is sometimes given to make me go faster, or if I've been naughty, a good few stripes across the buttocks can be expected. It isn't a heavy form of corporal punishment scene, but a little is enough to add to the level of obedience. I always try to do the best I can, be it in dressage or on the track. However, I do play up sometimes just to keep the trainers on their toes. Punishment is similar to submitting. I couldn't just bend over for a crack across my bum just because I was told to. However, with my harness on, if the trainer wants me to bend over they should be able to make me. I also feel that hitting for the sake of it wouldn't be as much fun as if it was in a training context. If the trainer deems it necessary to punish, it should be hard enough to be a real lesson.

I have about four or five sessions a year as a pony. Certainly not as much time as I would like. A typical session lasts three hours. The yearly treat is 'ponying' in public on the SM Pride march through London. I also spend some time making tack and helping build pony carts.

I don't take on the psychological aspects of the role play too much. That is, I don't mentally 'become' a pony while I'm playing. I'm simply a girl being forced to act like a pony for the pleasure and amusement of others. But, having said that, you do find yourself be-having like a real pony might. I also get a real kick about being put in a stable. In particular, I like sleeping in the stable overnight, as I get to be chained up. Not for me a clip on a halter, being a human used as a pony I could simply unclip it. In the stable my harness is removed, and my 'stable shackles' applied. There is a ring bolted to the wall in the stall about three feet from the ground. My chains have a padlock brazed to the end that fix on the ring. A second lock attaches to the back of the collar, then the chain continues down to the feet, which are secured with ankle cuffs. It's finished with two chains coming through the legs at crotch level, also attached to the main chain, with a separated pair of handcuffs on the end. When I lay on my back my arms can just rest at my side, and the whole thing is therefore very secure but quite comfortable.

I mostly enjoy all the aspects of being treated like an animal. It's quite impersonal and humiliating. Also I love being shown off as a pretty creature in front of others or being forced to work like a pony. I also enjoy the fact that other people, not just my owner, might choose to ride me or take me for a canter and there's little I can do to resist. But, as I said, I don't actually imagine I'm a pony, just a girl being treated like a pony or being forced to act like one.

Most of the people I've spoken to about pony play share the same basic idea, whether they be male or female. There are a few who 'pretend' to be real ponies reincarnated, but they don't tend to stay in role for long. I would say my experience is quite intense. After an hour or two in role, I'm emotionally relaxed and not thinking about normal life at all. By this point, I am just a beast of burden. I have stayed in role all day on occasions, and the psychological and emotional effects have lasted for several days.

My typical day as a pony would start off in the stable, naked, shut in a stall. My Mistress enters carrying the tack which she dresses me in, bridle first to make sure I can't speak. Arms are bound behind the back and a strong harness fitted over my hips. Only then do I feel 'controlled'. The less I know of the 'programme', if there is one, the better. Once prepared, I'm then led from the stable on a leading rein up to the dressage ring where I have to walk, trot or canter in circles on command. The whip is ever present if I'm not lifting my legs high enough or holding my head back proudly. Mistress might try a few of the more complex moves, or even jumps. She always praises me when I'm doing well.

Once warmed up, I'm shackled into one of the single pony carts. At first it can be quite hard to pull, but after a while my muscles get used to it. I breath heavily, straining against my bounds on the up hill sections, then recover as we canter back downhill. All the time, I'm being directed by the bit in my mouth and the whip on my exposed buttocks. Between periods of riding, I'm tethered securely to a post or fence. It's most relaxing to have nothing to do but watch the wildlife or the other ponies. If it's a cold day, you hope one of the riders or stable hands will put a pony blanket over you to keep you warm. I can drink from the horse trough and quietly recover my energy before someone else wants to take me for a trot. I dread being driven while wearing a blindfold. Though I trust my Mistress not to let me walk into a tree or ditch, I find it hard to keep up a reasonable pace. Only practice will improve this.

At some stage, I may be tethered into the big carriage with one or more of the other ponies. We have to work together, keeping in step and being aware of each others position on the narrower sections of track. At the end of the session, I'll be watered and then led back to the stable where my harness, but not my arm bindings and bridle, are removed. At last I can lay down on the soft warm hay, take the weight off my hoofs and rest my aching legs.

How far would I dream of this role going? I would love to trot my Mistress to the shops and the pub, and be kept in role for several days on end, but it could get boring not being able to talk and I couldn't imagine doing it for a week!

Chapter 15: Sally

Age: 32, Location: Berkshire, United Kingdom

I have no wish to endanger my relationship with my husband. We also have a six year old and a baby, so my playing away from home is a bit inhibited until they're older. We have a relationship of equals and it's very good. But I do need to fulfil this other side of me where I'm a slut who's used for pleasure. I couldn't bring up this kind of subject with my husband, and I wouldn't want to. I have mentioned threesomes to him but he recoiled in horror at the idea so I pretended it was just pure fantasy and that I'd never want to do anything like that for real.

In fact, I'd never been with another man before my husband and never had an affair until I got involved with soldiers. I live near an army base and I've always liked men in uniform anyway. I met my first soldier at a night club on a girls night out. He was married, so he had to be as discreet as me. I had an affair with him for four years. I need to be with a very dominant man before my submissive slut side comes out, which is why I could never do anything like this with my husband. You can't get much more dominant than a professional soldier. He trained me up as if we were in boot camp. I'd have to strip on command as quickly as I could and be timed while I was doing it. I'd have to stand to attention and be given a good dressing down on all my faults. I love to be verbally abused by men. As I am quite a large person a lot of the abuse is about my size. For some reason I love being insulted and belittled, especially laughed at. It's weird I know but I simply adore men calling me names and telling me to wiggle my big fat arse for their entertainment.

When I'm in what I call 'submissive head space' I will do absolutely anything for the dominant man I'm with. But he has to be genuinely dominant, not play acting. There is something about a brutal guy that is very exciting for me. I know I have no choice but to do what I'm told. If I didn't I know he would think nothing of telling me to fuck off. He'd probably throw me out the front door stark naked and throw my clothes after me. I've been made to do things which later I've been thoroughly ashamed of, but I know I'll always go back for more. I've licked men's bottoms and been used as a toilet on many occasions. On one occasion he even shoved his turd up my pussy.

Before I met my master I did dabble quite a bit in self abuse, such as spanking and whipping myself in front of the mirror and putting myself into self bondage. Obviously, this fulfilled a need in part, but was in no way equal to the real thing. Nowadays I still continue with self abuse but under my master's guidance. Sometimes this is done over the phone. As we are both married our times together are limited and infrequent. Out of necessity and in order to keep the momentum and dynamics going when we are apart, we'll indulge in a lot of phone sex. If I'm at home alone, he'll order me to do things like play with myself over the phone or, one of his favourites, is to order me to place the phone between my bum cheeks and spank myself. Another favourite is to listen to me in the toilet, which I find both exciting and extremely embarrassing. Most embarrassing of all though is when he calls me on my mobile while I'm going round the shops or something. I've almost orgasmed a few times going round the supermarket pushing the trolley before now. Listening to him abuse and insult me in a public place is incredible.

After six months or so of regular sessions, he decided to introduce me to his friend, another soldier. It was really horny how it was done. I met John as usual for an afternoon session and he suddenly announced his mate was downstairs and that he wanted to bring him up. I'd never been naked in front of two guys before and, I must say, I found the situation very exiting; especially when he gave me to his mate to use, that really blew my mind! That whole idea of being someone's sexual property is something I love. He watched while I unzipped Bill and gave him a good blow job. Then he asked John if it was alright if he raped me and John gave his permission. I wasn't even consulted to see if it was what I wanted. I was just a slut, and I loved every minute of it.

My biggest fantasy involves being abused to the point of rape. Luckily, my soldier friends are very willing to indulge this fantasy. My favourite scenario is to have both men take me. One will grab me from behind and put his hand over my mouth and warn me not to scream. The other will rip my blouse open and tear apart the clips of my bra, exposing my very large breasts. He will then smack my tits back and forth very hard. All the time he does this he will be keeping up a constant barrage of verbal abuse, of course. I absolutely adore having my tits slapped hard and very roughly man handled. They will tear off all my clothes till I'm completely naked. By the way, this is all prearranged, so I'll know to bring an extra set of clothes to wear home afterwards. Next they'll force me face up against a wall so one can rape my bottom standing up. They then force me onto the floor and take their belts off and whip me all over. My favourite punishment scenario, incidentally, is to be forced to kneel at a coffee table with my tits on the table top. They will then be caned and whipped very severely.

Obviously, we have to go easy with punishment as I can't afford to show any marks when I go home, of course. Fortunately, my husband has to work away from home for several weeks at a time in his job. If the whipping happens at the beginning of this period it allows the marks to go down by the time he returns.

After the beating I will be dragged along the floor by my ankles, spread-eagled and then forced to lick their bottoms while they take turns squatting over me. Another double penetration rape will invariably follow. They've both shit on me and pissed in my mouth. Most importantly, neither of them has ever asked if it was something I wanted, they just go ahead and do their worst, or best, depending on how you look at it!

At the moment I am waiting for them to fulfil one promise, or threat, which is to sneak me into the barracks and be used by a whole barrack room full of soldiers. There are a lot of girls who love men in uniform, as I do. Apparently, some of the girls go to extreme lengths to fuck soldiers, according to John and Bill. Like climbing over the barbed wire perimeter fence, just so they can fuck the guys. John told me one story about these two girls, who couldn't have been more than eighteen. They got taken to the barrack room and worked their way done all the bunk beds, fucking all the guys. Now that's what I'm dying to try!

Chapter 16: Nicki

Age: 34, Location: London

Funnily enough, I was never interested in school uniforms or anything like that when I actually was at school. Though I suppose I was always a bit theatrical and enjoyed dressing up. Oh, and I've always loved being spanked, of course. My interest started a few years ago when I read about adult school boys and school girls in a magazine somewhere.

The idea really took hold of my imagination, especially the dramatic aspects of acting out the role. The problem was I had no one to play with. My husband has always been very broad minded and understanding but, unfortunately, when it comes to role play he prefers the submissive role too. As I could no more dominate him than he me, this was a very real problem for us for a while. Eventually, we decided that in order to fulfil this aspect of our personalities we would have to go our separate ways, sexually, that is. So we set about finding people who would like to join us. Neither of us wanted an affair as such, just role playing partners.

There are plenty of dominatrices around, both life style and professional, so it was comparatively easy for him to find what he wanted. For me, however, it proved to be a good deal harder. I answered adverts in sex contact magazines, and even put in a few myself. Although I got lots and lots of replies and offers, I found the vast majority were from men who were basically interested in beating up women, which is not what I was after at all. There are some pretty sick individuals out there and, for a woman who is interested in the submissive role it can be potentially very dangerous. One method we found to sort out the wheat from the chaff was to insist they meet both myself and my husband together on a social level first. As you can imagine the dubious element were put off straight away. In this way my husband meets and approves the 'teachers' who I have sessions with. They will come round to the house for a chat first. No sessions take place in my home as my husband doesn't really want to see me in that situation. Actually, people who know me in this scene would be very surprised, or shocked I should say, if they knew what I was like in everyday life. I'm actually considered very strait-laced and prim and proper. In fact, I even sing in my local church choir!

I've always been attracted to older men for these games and could never imagine letting myself be spanked by someone my own age or younger. They just wouldn't fit into my idea of a 'teacher'. My school age is around fourteen. As I said, sex doesn't usually come into this scenario, though sometimes a bit of a sexy element will creep in. One case in particular stands out and that was with a gentleman who I would prefer to remain nameless. He really took the whole spanking experience into another realm for me by introducing character and situations into our play. For instance, he would ask the most gorgeously embarrassing questions about what I had been doing hanging round the boys changing rooms at school. I would then have to confess that I'd been playing with the boys cocks or showing myself off for sweets or pocket money or something like that. The scenario would get really filthy. We will invent particular boy characters with whom I'm supposed to be getting up to all sorts of mucky things. We'll give them names and everything. Another favourite of his is to have me write down all the sexual fantasies I've had since our last meeting, especially those involving 'teacher'. He also delights in giving me psychical examinations and will punish me if I show any signs of sexual arousal. You can imagine I get quite a bit of punishment!

I have toyed with the idea of doing this on a professional basis. I have done one or two spanking clubs and parties, which have been fun. They normally take place in the afternoons because the majority of devotees of spanking are retired gentlemen. The venues are normally private houses rather than clubs. It's much nicer because one can create a very genteel atmosphere with afternoon tea being served. It wouldn't be the same in a night club situation. Usually the houses are detached properties and very discreet. The trouble with spanking is that it is a very noisy sport and the sound does carry. I really like playing the maid role sometimes at these events. Of course, I'll get spanked if I drop a spoon whilst serving the men, but that's all part of the game. These events are quite small with usually no more than ten or a dozen men and maybe two or three girls. Sometimes it will go beyond spanking and there will be a lot of hands up skirts and fingering. Once or twice I've been at parties where it has ended up with one or more of the girls being gang banged. But this will only happen if the girl wants it. The men are generally very nice and won't do anything the girl doesn't want. Everyone is very aware of the correct way to spank a girl and the organisers keep a close eye on the girls safety.

The professional submissive girls at these clubs are very hard and must have bums like elephant hide. They do get paid a lot of money to be caned and spanked. After all, they end up so bruised they wouldn't be able to work for weeks afterwards. The men at these clubs don't want to spank a bruised bum. They must have a girl with no marks. I couldn't do this as a career the way they do. I do this for fun really, not for money. Though the extra cash comes in handy.

Chapter 17: Pam

Age: 20, Location: Nottingham, United Kingdom

I am very submissive by nature and have been given the name of a slut because I need and get a lot of sex. While growing up in Nottingham, I went to school with a lot of black children. I have always been sexually drawn to black boys who are very forceful by nature and verbally vulgar.

Maybe I take after my mother. When I was younger my father once caught her being fucked in our house by our black window cleaner. She has been into black men ever since. I was 16 when she took up with a younger black boyfriend and let him move in with us. His friend, another black man, was always with him and both men used to take my mother up to the bedroom in the afternoons. I used to hear her moaning and groaning in ecstasy as I lay in my bedroom. Needless to say, this always made me feel very sexy and I'd wish it was me having all that fun!

One afternoon I was to get my chance with them. My mother was out at work and I was alone in my room when I heard the two of them come home. I knew they were outside my door looking through the keyhole. We lived in a house that still had those big old fashioned keyholes, although the keys had long since disappeared. They couldn't see anything, but I knew they were there trying to get a glimpse of me and I could hear them giggling and whispering suggestively to each other about what they'd like to do to me. I felt incredibly excited and my heart was racing.

They went downstairs and a moment later called up to me with orders to make them tea and sandwiches. Naturally, I was eager to obey their demands. My excitement mounted as I slipped into my shortest mini skirt (no panties!) Long woollen stockings that came up over the knee and a tight fitting tee shirt with no bra. I wanted them both to be in no doubt as to what I wanted and needed! I have to admit I was already wet and eager as I went downstairs and felt their eyes stripping me!

After fixing them something to eat, I announced I was going to take a bath. Going back upstairs, I moved my bed so that if they were to look through the keyhole again it would be in line. My heart was pounding as I stripped and went naked from my bedroom to the bathroom. At first I locked the door, but then felt so turned on and daring that I slid back the bolt again. All the while I was having my bath I expected them to walk in, but they didn't. After I finished drying myself, I again felt a dangerous thrill run through my body and a tightening of my stomach muscles as I faced the risk of returning naked to my bedroom.

I was brushing my hair as I left the bathroom. At that moment their heads appeared over the bannisters; a wave of excitement coursed up my spine and I froze just looking at them while, all open mouthed and wide eyed, they drank in the sight of my nakedness. As my senses jumped back into gear, I deliberately dropped the hairbrush and, turning my back on them, slowly bent over to pick it up, giving them an uninterrupted view of my now wet sex in the process. I then calmly straightened up and minced provocatively back to my room. Once the door was closed I jumped on the bed face down with my legs wide apart.

My mouth was dry and my heart almost exploding as I heard them once more moving about just outside my door. I knew they were looking through the keyhole again, only this time they could see everything. A voice inside my head kept screaming: "come in, please, come in!" But they seemed to be standing there ages, whispering conspiratorially together. I began to fear they would never make a move, so I turned over on my back and spread my legs even wider and started to play with myself. Finally, the door to my bed-room slowly opened. I thought I would die of excitement as the two black men strolled, arrogantly grinning, across the room toward my bed. One stood leaning over my face, while the other sat on the bed beside me and, roughly pushing my hand aside, pushed his own thick fingers into my dripping vagina and started rubbing vigorous-ly. I turned to look up at the first man and saw to my delight that he had already unzipped his fly and let his swollen manhood stood out like an enormous black monster, demanding me to give it pleasure. Obediently, I closed my eyes, raised my face toward it and opened my mouth wide. The rock hard flesh entered my willing mouth at the same moment as the second man's cock thrust into my aching vagina. I have no words to describe the waves of sheer pleasure that run through my wild, heaving body as unforgiving hands mauled at my tender breasts and nipples. Verbal abuse broke the sweaty silence with things like: "Come on, you fucking slut, work that ass!"

I lost all concept of time, but they must have used me non-stop for two hours or more. Changing ends with each other often, they must have man handled me into every position possible. From doggy to wheelbarrow, to flat on my back with my legs touching my ears. As all the time I was ordered and encouraged with more verbal abuse to move my body and act more and more like a slave-slut.

My whole body seemed to be on fire with lust as sweat ran off me and I heard myself screaming, "Fuck me, fuck me", until my mouth was once more plugged with cock. I felt the gush of hot, thick cum shoot down my throat and soon after another full load of the stuff was shot all over my bottom and back as the men moaned and shouted at me.

All the strength had now gone from my body and I just flopped down on the bed exhausted. My brain was in a trance. I tried to move my aching body to relieve the tingling feeling in my vagina. The men were now doing up their pants and leaving the room as I weakly begged them to stay and fuck me more. It seemed I lay there for hours, cold on the outside but burning up inside, with my back and bottom all sticky with cum. I eventually forced myself to get up and walk back to the bathroom where I literally flopped into the tub once more. When I got out I hadn't even the strength to dry myself, so I just staggered back to the bedroom naked. As I pushed open the door I saw my two black lovers sitting naked on the bed slowly playing with their erect cocks. "Come on, you fucking slut," one said, proudly displaying his weapon for me to worship, "Get your ass in here."

These steamy sessions went on for months and it appeared, one or both, of these men had told others about me because I got a lot of attention from black men in my area. I heard a lot of things said about me, too. Okay, it was true. But, I'm not ashamed of being a submissive slut. I think of myself as just a healthy young female who needs a lot of cock from very forceful and very well endowed black men who know how to service me well. Unfortunately, my mother found out about me and her boyfriends and ordered me to leave home.

I had already met another very big black guy from Bristol in a bar one night. He told me he photographed girls nude and had asked me to model for him. At the time I had refused as I was deeply involved in my secret (or so I thought) sex romps. I remembered he had given me his address in case I ever changed my mind. Searching through my things I eventually found it and, without saying a word to anyone, I left home and headed for Bristol.

Arriving at his house, I rang the bell and waited. Eventually, a white girl answered the door and asked me what I wanted. I told her I was looking for a guy called Winston.

"Mr. Winston to you." She corrected me.

Well, it turned out Mr Winston had this girl living with him as his slave, but he took me round to one of his black friends who also took pictures of girls and there I lived for over a year as his personal sex slave. This man was very dominant and very much into the leather scene. I learned an awful lot from him. As my Master, he took me to some clubs in Amsterdam and I found I enjoyed it.

Things change and my Master met a blonde girl with a ginger pussy hair and she became his number one slave. I wouldn't say I was thrown out, but let's just say he didn't want to stop me leaving and said so. I moved out and came to London where I modelled for mainly Asian and black photographers and many white guys, too. I am more than ever drawn to very dominant black men and have been with many. I am not bothered by age or looks as long as they have what I need—a dominant nature and a very big cock. At the moment I am living with a Nigerian in his forties' who is hung like a horse. He is verbally obscene and abusive to me with stamina to match. I obey his wishes totally as he has an attitude I respect. I am not saying I will stay with him forever, but until such time as we part he has everything I need in a lover and a Master.

Chapter 18: Valerie

Age: 43, Location: London, United Kingdom

It has only been since my divorce and after my children were all grown and flown that I have had the chance to explore my own submissive tendencies and fantasies of being a slave to the full. As a black woman and, as far as I know, the only black woman on the scene as a slave girl, this opens up a whole can of worms for me, both personally and culturally. This would be something I would never be able to discuss with any one from my own West Indian culture. It would an understatement to say they would be completely shocked at my actually wanting to return to a historical state my people suffered for centuries. Remember, our people were in chains for real and it wasn't sexy at all!

Where this slave thing comes from and how it got into my head I just don't know. Maybe only a professional shrink could sort that one out! All I know is that right from childhood I was always fascinated and, though I didn't realise it at the time, very aroused by images in history books of black women in chains under the whip of cruel white master on those plantations.

I first got to know masters on chatlines and met up with a few. Most were disappointments, I'm afraid. They were little more than wannabe dominants who were fine abusing me on the phone, but in real life didn't have a clue. Only one man I met in this way came up anywhere near my expectations. After many lengthy phone conversations, we arranged to meet. Luckily, he lived fairly close, but not too close, to where I live. We arranged to meet on neutral ground. But not, I'm glad to say anywhere as naff as a restaurant or bar. Oh no, he took the helm straight away in picking up on one of my fantasies I'd discussed; that is, outdoor scenarios. I'd always loved anonymous sex outdoors and had already experienced the car park scene with previous boyfriends.

He decided our first session would take place at a secluded woodland spot about ten miles from me. The scenario would run like this: I was to come along at midnight in my car, wearing only a long coat and be stark naked underneath. I was to park at a certain spot known as a hang out for gays and swingers and wait for him to approach me. As I had no idea what he looked like or exactly what was expected of me, the whole thing had the wonderful edge of excitement to it. I know a lot of people who will eventually be reading this will think women like me are completely mad to do the things we do. They are probably quite right. I can't explain the need, but the danger is like a drug to me.

I waited in the area for about five minutes before another car pulled up a short distance away. My heart almost leaped into my mouth as this man got out and started to walk in a very determined manner toward me. I realised immediately this was the master I was supposed to meet. I quickly slipped out of my coat and sat waiting for him completely naked with just my collar and chain around my neck. Actually, I was supposed to have been naked all the while but the truth was I was too scared to do that and figured he'd never know anyway if I was a little disobedient.

He took command straight away and ordered me to follow him. He didn't even look back to see if I was doing what I was told. The fact that he just assumed I was doing his bidding was, I thought, pretty cool. He made me follow him down this country path and then off into the woods. Remember, this in the middle of the fucking night with a complete stranger and I'm stark naked! We had some wonderful fun that first night. He made me run across a field and then tied me to a tree and fucked me after giving me a very sound whipping with his belt. That was a couple of years ago and we are still friends and play together whenever possible. I have gone on and met some other dominant men since then, though I've never met one that I would want to commit to full time.

Perhaps the most shocking aspect of all this is the thrill it gives me to be racially abused by my white masters. I love it when they call me a black bitch or a black whore or when they tell me to get my big fat black ass over here. When my current master throws parties I am always required to wait on table and serve all his dominant friends in the role of maid. I even have a uniform for this role. I am punished for the slightest mistake like dropping a spoon or putting things in the wrong place on the dining table. The men are also allowed to put their hands up my skirt and fondle my backside whenever they want to. I am, of course, never allowed to wear knickers at all. Sometimes, after the men have finished eating, I have to crawl under the table and give each man in turn a blow job.

Another kind of party my master holds is his slave auctions where, obviously, I am the slave on the auction block. Knowing my fantasy, master tries to make it as much like the genuine slave auctions I'd read about and seen pictures of as he can. I am led in naked and in chains and paraded around the room so the men can access the goods up for sale. During all this I am treated like some kind of farm yard animal. My lips are pulled back and my teeth and gums examined. My tits are pulled and squeezed. My pussy is groped and I'm ordered to turn round and spread my bum cheeks so that they can even examine intimately my arse hole. After this I am ordered to stand naked on a chair while the men make bids for me. What they are bidding for is the right to take me home with them and use me for the night.

The third and most extreme kind of party is when I am locked in a room while the men talk and drink in the next room. Whenever the fancy takes them, one or more will come in and use me in whatever way they wish. There are no limits. For the most part, in between sex and beating, I am used as a human toilet. Sometimes I am in the room for a whole weekend. I am not allowed to wash myself or anything. By the end of one of these long sessions I feel completely defiled, yet complete. That is pretty much my life as a slave so far and I wouldn't change any of it.

Chapter 19: Wendy

Age: 41, Location, Chester, United Kingdom

I am a submissive female. I am an extreme masochist. I am also completely blind. If people aren't shocked by the first two statements, they are by the third. Even experienced scene players recoil in horror at the thought of abusing a disabled person. Which makes me angry, as it is just another example of the way society excludes us. If I want to be beaten and abused as part of my sexual identity, why shouldn't I? Of course, I realised from the outset the dangers involved in this kind of level of play but, at the end of the day, I have come to the conclusion that it is a risk well worth taking in order to fulfil myself.

Ever since I can remember—even before I lost my sight at the age of twelve—my fantasies have always revolved round themes of brutal sex, kidnappings, group rape and even full time slavery. While other girls might have dreamt about being a ballerina, I always fantasised about being someone's property. I must have been only around eight or nine, but I still wanted to be a sex object to be used; even though there wasn't any real sex involved in my early fantasies, just lots of groping and touching-up. I would love to read about places like Ancient Rome or watch films like Spartacus or Ben Hur and always wondered what the slaves were complaining about! It seemed like submissive heaven to me. I would happily dream about being used and abused by my Roman masters for hours on end. As a masochist, too, I've even had sexual fantasies about being tortured and crucified!

Even at that age, the boys at my school picked up on the way I was. They soon knew that they could do anything with me that they wanted and I wouldn't object. When we played Doctors and Nurses I would always be the patient who got stripped and examined. And when the boys played at war games, it was always me who was taken prisoner. When that happened I would be told to strip and the boys would fiddle about with me, though they didn't really know what they were doing, of course. Sometimes they would get their little cocks out and I'd have to play with them. Once, I remember, I was taken prisoner and tied up, then locked in the boot of a car for the whole afternoon!

While I may be blind and I may be submissive, I am not stupid. I do have a ten year old child and I need to keep her safe. But as long as I know that she isn't exposed to any dangers, then what happens to my own body is my business and my responsibility. I keep her out of this completely and she doesn't have any idea what goes on. At least, I hope she doesn't. Naturally, I worry what might happen to her if the worst occurred and I did end up being murdered as the result of my adventures. But it's not something I have any power to do anything about. I am addicted to this lifestyle now, and wouldn't be able to change, even if I wanted to.

I was married for six years to a wonderful and very kind man who would do anything for me—except, unfortunately, the one thing I wanted above all else. He looked after me completely but, in the end, it all became just too suffocating. I certainly wasn't able to express any of this side of myself. In fact, it was just the opposite. If anything, he wanted me to be the dominant one. Which just isn't where I'm coming from at all! It's always been the same with all my boyfriends, I'm afraid. They have all been infuriating nice! Because of my disability people in general seem to be incapable of treating me the way I want to be treated—which is very brutal.

In the end, I had to resort to finding the kind of partner I needed in the only way I knew how given my circumstances. And that was through the Internet and phone chat lines. This was a wonderful outlet for me. It gives you the chance to be whoever and whatever you want to be. Surprisingly, there are very few dominant men on these lines. Most want to be Submissives themselves. It took a lot of determination and a lot of time to establish contact with the right kind of men.

My first experience was with a policeman who I had been chatting to for several months on one of these sex chat lines. He was married and had a daughter not much older than me who he had often interfered with as a child. As she had grown into womanhood as a teenager his relationship with her deteriorated and he had to look elsewhere for fun with young girls. His ideas were very cruel and vicious and included fantasies of cutting off my nipples and cunt lips with a razor. I was terrified and hooked at the same time by all this. I had never heard such brutal things before.

I'll never forget that first time with him. I must admit there were moments when, as I prepared myself for our rendezvous that I almost lost my nerve and stood him up. But I knew this what I wanted more than anything else in the world and what I was born for. It may sound a bit grand and pretentious to say it, but I really felt like I was meeting my destiny in some strange way.

We met at a café in the centre of my home town. At least I was on familiar ground up until this point and could get myself there under my own steam. I sat myself down at a table and waited for my date to arrive, pretending to drink a cup of tea, but actually trembling too much to even attempt to pick up the cup. I'd described myself to him (there can't have been many women in the café with a white stick!) So he knew who to look for. After all, he'd have to be the one who found me, wasn't he?

After what seemed like an age I felt the presence of someone standing over me and heard that voice that had become so familiar to me after so many hours of conversation on the telephone. He asked if I was Wendy. I managed to stammer out that I was and, without any more formalities, he leaned down till his mouth was at my ear and whispered that I was to stand up immediately and come with him. Naturally, in my state of mind, I didn't think twice about obeying him. In the street he took my arm and escorted me to the

car. On the way he didn't say a word. He didn't need to. The circum-
stances of my 'kidnap' had been well worked out in minute detail
on the phone weeks before. We'd wanked together many times over
every phase of my abuse and I knew he intended to take me to an
isolated country spot he knew and rape me in every orifice. Before
that he was going to beat my tits and cunt thoroughly. At the end of
the session I was to be dropped off back in town so I could make my
own way home.

And that's exactly what happened! In all, I suppose this liai-
son lasted about six months until it got to the stage where I became
bored with the repetition of events and it just wasn't exciting me anymore. He was what I call a 'one joke master' in that his methods of
using me were unchanging, unimaginative and without variation in
the slightest detail. He liked raping me in fields, tying me to trees and
beating my tits which, while I love all of that, can get a bit tedious—
too much of a good thing, as they say! So one day, I simply stopped
seeing him or taking his calls. He had never found out where I lived
(I'm not that stupid!) So he had no way of finding me.

Incidentally, to anyone who doesn't understand how this
scene works, the submissive actually has the last word and is ultimately in control in a bizarre convoluted way. If she, or he, doesn't
like the way she is being used then they will simply stop submitting! It's something that the normal non-scene people can't seem to
get their heads around.

Sense of smell touch and, of course, anticipation are all en-
hanced for me. As a regular feature of any scenario a master puts
me through, I love it when he makes me shit, for instance, and then
holds my head an inch over the mess and makes me sniff it while
telling me what a dirty bitch I am.

I can't explain why I need to put myself in such dangerous situation. Even some of my previous masters have been shocked by what
I've been through and the extremes I'm prepared to go. One master
remarked that he wouldn't be at all surprised to read in the news-
papers about me being murdered and found in the river. But the
danger involved in meeting brutal strangers is the attraction and the

turn-on for me.

I do have a regular master at the moment. Again he is married, so our games can only take place at irregular intervals. He isn't going to leave his wife and, even if he did, he's not interested in having a master and slave lifestyle all the time, which is what I want. This isn't the ideal situation, but it will have to do until I find a full time master.

My master is quite keen on group sex and gang bang scenarios, which I enjoy very much. During these scenes involving other people I am always blindfolded, so the men don't realise that I really can't see. In these scenarios I am usually left for considerable periods of time in a room on my own. I am stripped and shackled to the wall by my neck. Sometimes I'm left for hours with only a bucket to piss in and a dog bowl to drink water from. The idea is that I have to wait till my master comes back with his dominant male friends from the pub or wherever they are. I find it incredibly thrilling, that sense of anticipation. When they arrive, they won't come in straight away. I can hear them laughing and joking in the living room. I know they are talking about me. It's a real turn on. By the time I hear the door open and them come into the room, I am in a fever pitch of excitement.

I love hearing them talk about me as if I'm not there, or like I'm a dumb animal that's being shown off, a thing to be used. I know they will be naked now and, by the breathless sound of their voices, playing with themselves, as well. By the time my master finally touches me, it is like a minor electric shock. Being blind really does heighten all your other senses, which makes for fantastic scenes.

I am made to give all the men a circle suck. This is where I have to kneel and the guys stand around me, maybe five or six, and I have to suck them all in turn. The best part of the game is that I have to guess by the taste and smell which is my master's cock. I always know which one is his, but sometimes I will guess wrong on purpose just to experience the beating he'll give me.

Master also lends me out to individual dominant men for an hour or day or even sometimes a whole weekend. On these occasions I am never told who I'm going to meet or where I'll be taken. All I know is that, because whoever it is has been vouched for by Master, I will be abused but safely returned home at the end of the session. The pattern is usually the same. I'm told to be in a certain meeting place at such and such a time. There I wait for my new master to approach me and spirit me away to wherever! I've ended up in some pretty bizarre situations, I can tell you!

I've also been used in car parks and men's public toilets, which is one of my master's favourites. My current master is bisexual, which is great for me because I'd always fantasised about what guys get up to with each other, especially in toilets. From what I'd heard they never had any problem getting casual sex. It always seemed a bit sad and unfair that women aren't as up front about it as that.

I knew my master had been picking up men in gents toilets since he was about fourteen and had told me some really horny stories about it. Like the time he had stripped off his school uniform while four or five dirty old men in their seventies took turns sucking his cock and licking his bum. I could easily imagine my arrogant master, even as a young boy, loving all that body worship.

The images in my mind of guys at it with each other like that really turned me on so much that I begged my Master to take me with him so that I could experience what went on for myself. He had told me that a lot of the men who frequent the toilets on a regular basis are actually bisexual, and many of them are married. According to my master, they go 'cottaging' because their own wives don't like sucking cock or taking anal sex. And, anyway, he said even the gay guys are still like the straight men in that they don't mind what gender is doing the sucking, just so long as they get sucked off by someone. So my mouth would be just as welcome as the guys!

That first time he took me to what, he claimed, was a famous loo for cottaging, I'd never been in a gents toilets before in my life and didn't realise how gross and evil smelling they were compared to the cleanliness of a ladies convenience. But, then again, that did add to the excitement and naughtiness of it all!

He forced me into one of the cubicles and ordered me to strip off completely. He then confiscated all my clothes, which he put into a hold-all and told me to lock myself in and wait for his command to come out. Meanwhile, he said he would stand at the trough where the men piss and make himself hard while he waited for the first guy to come in, which he informed me wouldn't be long at all. While I sat naked on the toilet seat in my tiny, smelly cell, the anticipation was almost unbearable. There's nothing more exciting than knowing you are going to be having sex with a complete stranger in a few minutes, and in such exquisitely sordid surroundings, too!

Sure enough, within a few minutes this man came in (he turned out to be a middle-aged business type). My Master told me later that he kept glancing at Master's stiff cock while he wanked himself up. By this time my pussy was on fire and I was rubbing myself furiously between my legs as I strained my ears to listen to what was going on. I could hear them whispering and they seemed very excited, but I couldn't make out what they were saying to each other. The next thing I knew there was a gentle tapping on the cubicle door, which I knew was the signal for my entrance into the proceedings! Terrified, but incredibly excited at the same time, I pulled back the latch and inched open the door to reveal my nakedness.

There was no mistaking the man's gasp of surprise when I opened that door. I must have seemed like an apparition to him. After all, he had gone into the toilets to have some cock fun with another guy probably because his own wife wouldn't do the business, and here he was being handed a real woman on a plate who was trained and ready to fulfil his wildest dreams!

With my Master's encouragement he came into the cubicle and began to touch me up. I could my Master asking him what he thought of his property (i.e. Me!) and what he'd like to do to it! While these negotiations were going on I was sitting on the toilet seat rubbing both cocks round my face and slipping each in turn into my mouth. Sometimes the scenario would end up with me being pissed on or tied up to the toilet cistern. Often in the course of events I'd be used by up to seven or eight men in turn. These toilets were like rush hour on the underground sometimes! If a particular man turned out to have a penchant for dominance, my Master would give him a contact phone number and he would be invited to join his network of dominants.

In car parks it is very different to the toilet scene. There is a distinct message code for letting guys know that a couple is up for sex. It really is a definite sub-culture. All its own. You have to know where the car parks are. They are scattered all around the country and people come from a long way to meet up. Mostly it is a gay scene but many swingers also use them for meet ups. There is a complex system of flashing lights to indicate who is up for fun.

I've never had an orgasm from normal sex. The only way I can orgasm is through being whipped. If you're not a masochist you wouldn't understand the effect a whipping has on you. You go into yourself and can get a really out of the body experience through the pain. Like most Submissives, I take pride in the punishment I can take. It's a way of letting the world know how much attention my master gives me and how well he's trained me. A submissive wears her bruises like medals.

Ultimately, I need to be in slavery twenty-four seven. I realise this will have to wait until my daughter is grown up and doesn't need me anymore. I haven't found a master yet who is willing to go the whole way. For most in the scene, it is just a game. Something they play at once a month when they put on their fetish gear and go out to a club. For me, it is my whole life, and I yearn for the day when I can make it the basis of my existence.

Chapter 20: Rachel

Age: 30, Location: Chertsey, United Kingdom

Let's take a walk, you and me. I can see you're surprised when you see me coming. From my photograph, I look quite respectable, don't I? I look very different now. I'm wearing my highest black patent stiletto heels, seamed black, silk stockings; black suspender belt; my tiniest g-string knickers; a very short mini skirt and a thin see-through top. I'm also wearing thick, bright red lipstick. In fact, I've purposefully made myself up to look like a cheap backstreet whore! To complete the picture, I've put on an ankle chain to show everyone what a whore I am.

So, we take our little walk in the woods. When we are far enough into the trees so that no one can see us, you say: "Drop to your knees and kiss my shoes".

I stay down there, licking your shoes until they're spotless. You then allow me to undo your trousers and take out your penis. You tell me I have precisely five minutes to bring you to a climax using my mouth and bright red lips. I know that failure to make you come will be dealt with severely. If I am successful, I realise that I must earn the right to taste your spunk. And if you do come on this occasion, your hot sticky semen will be deposited all over my face, hair and tits.

Next, you inform me: "I'll teach you to dress like a tart when you come to see me."

You rip the clothes off me very roughly until I am standing before you stark naked. You take out a length of rope from under your coat and tie me to a tree with it. You then look around for a branch to whip my bottom and back with.

After my whipping it is time to go. But my clothes are lying in tatters on the ground, no use to anyone. You give me your coat and we walk back. The stones and twigs are hurting my bare feet, but you show no sign of sympathy. We get out of the woods and back onto the streets. There are people about and you love the fact that I am naked and vulnerable under your coat. I get some strange looks from people who see my dirty bare feet sticking out from under such a big man's overcoat. You keep making me bend over so that men can see my boobs. And reaching up, did the hem of the coat ride up enough to show my bare bottom?

This is a typical exciting encounter for me—when the mood takes, it's always very easy to find plenty of willing participants online!

THE END

If you enjoyed this book, you may also like to read the following abridged sample from 'Dominatrix', also available from Magnolia Books.

www.magnolia-books.com

Chapter 21: Mistress Mai-Ling

A Chinese psychiatric nurse from Singapore, turned professional dominatrix, Mai-Ling retired from the scene a year after this interview took place and is now running her own highly successful property development company in the midlands.

I first got into the scene by accident, really. I used to work in the field of psychiatric medicine. I had a friend of a friend who owned a studio. I was very dissatisfied with my job in the medical profession. I knew I wasn't going to get anywhere. I was looking for a way out when this fellow suggested I get into the S&M scene. I said: "What's that? What are you talking about?"

He offered to bring round a few magazines to show me. He also asked me if I wanted to go to a party that Saturday. Remember, I didn't know anything at this point. I didn't even have any clothes. I had to borrow some from the Mistress of the House where the party was being held. I decided not to think about anything. I thought I'd just leave my mind a blank and go with a completely open mind about things.

I was introduced to the people there as a 'Mistress in the Making', and I'd reply that I was thinking about it. I spoke to a transsexual mistress called Sadie and she was really nice. She told me to stick by her throughout the evening and I'd learn a thing or two. She showed me how to use the whip and all of that. Though, to be honest, watching all these people walking around half naked, I was secretly thinking: "Oh, no. This isn't my scene at all!"

At one point, as I was sitting down, someone said to me: "Mistress, can I be your footstool?" So, I said, rather casually: "Okay, yeah." He lifts my feet up and lays them across his naked back. I had really high heels on and I didn't want to hurt him. I didn't even realise at this point that, that was what he wanted more than anything in the world. But he said: "It's alright, Mistress, dig them in a little deeper." Well, if that's what he wants, I thought, okay. But I was also bursting to go to the toilet and I was wondering: "What do I do now?" The drink was beginning to go to my head, so I just kicked him and said: "Out of my way, I'm going for a pee". And he said: "Oh, Mistress, may I accompany you to the toilet?" I didn't have a clue to what to say to that, so I simply shouted: "How dare you!"

Later, the man who took me to the party asked me how I was getting on and I told him about the fellow and what had happened. And he just fell about laughing and said: "Why didn't you just piss on him and make him drink it?" I said: "What! Why should I?" Well, according to him that's what you should do. I didn't know! Anyway, that party was my introduction to the world of Fem-Dom. I soon got the hang of it, though. In fact, the very next day, the same guy phoned me up and asked me to go round to his house the next weekend and try my hand as a mistress. I said: "I don't think so, it's too much for me. I can't whip people like that."

Look at it from my point of view. I was very straight. I'd never dressed up, never done anything like that. I didn't know anything at all. But he was very insistent that I should go and see this other mistress and watch how she worked. So I went along when she had one of her regular slaves with her. Remember, this is the time I'd ever walked into a dungeon. I said: "What's this, for heavens sake?" He replied, very matter-of-factly: "This is a dungeon and this is a slave. And these are the weights you put on his balls."

He went on like this, talking about all the things they use. Then the mistress took over and told me to watch her whip the slave's backside, saying that I could take over later. When I took over, I hit him a few times and the slave started complaining, saying: "Mistress,

I don't think she's doing it hard enough." The mistress told me I had to really give it to him. So, I thought to myself: "Okay, I will!" I really started whacking him harder after that! But still not too hard because the blood put me right off, you know.

Afterwards, I asked the mistress if that was it? Was there anything else I needed to know? She said: "A lot. You've got to learn everything about this business. The best thing to do is to come and work with me now and again to get the hang of things." I didn't want to disappoint her, so I said alright. Later, I thought to myself: "Oh God, I've committed myself to something here! I don't know what I'm letting myself in for." Now and again I went down to see her and that's how I started to learn. But all the while, I was thinking: "I really can't do this. It's too harsh for me". Then my friend said: "I think you're looking at it from the wrong angle. There are other aspects to it. It's a big field that ranges from whipping to water sports". It was at the next party that I really started getting into domination. But it still took me another two years to build up enough courage to become a full-time mistress.

It was when I was on holiday in Italy that I thought to myself: "I think I'm going to go into that". When I came home I literally threw myself into it. I didn't think about anything else. I immediately made inquiries about taking a dungeon. By that time I'd seen a lot of videos and read a lot of books on the subject and felt ready. I gave a months notice at work and left. I knew this was something I wanted to do.

I still remember my very first client. He wanted a really good beating. I thought: "What shall I do? I'll just clear my mind and give it to him". And, amazingly enough, he came back for more! In fact, he ended up…

To read the rest get 'Dominatrix'
At Amazon from Magnolia Books.

'Dominatrix', explores the largely hidden world of the sado-masochistic female. The 20 selected interviews here were conducted over a 10-year period, by the BDSM magazine publisher and writer, Roy Turner. This eBook volume offers a full, frank and totally unique insight into the real world of the dominatrix, those who work within the 'sex industry', as well as those who live out the 'Fem-Dom' life-style in private.

What you get to hear is the authentic 'voice' of the women involved, how they got into it and the different techniques they employ to humiliate their male submissive clients/partners—way beyond the obvious strap-ons, canings and bondage clichés. Plus, what is also revealed is the effect their work has on their own personal lives and relationships, a rare glimpse 'behind the mask', as it were.

The genuine practitioner of Female Domination will take supreme pride in her skills and in her professionalism, and will disparage 'working girls' who clearly add the euphemism of 'personal services' to their menus (or the 'spank and wank brigade' as one interviewee succinctly put it) as being interlopers into her area of expertise and for giving her chosen vocation a bad name. A genuine, professional dominatrix or mistress/domme will never offer her client sexual favours. This 'no sex clause' is referred to again and again in these interviews as the yard stick by which to appraise the genuineness of a particular mistress.

Unlike a prostitute, who may be forced by circumstances to sell sex, the dominatrix sees herself as offering a legitimate service through her SM role-playing and fantasy skills that is very much on par with a therapist or counsellor. Indeed, the reader will note how similar the language of the dominatrix is to that of these other professionals. Interestingly, many come from the field of nursing, psychiatric or other caring services; including some who actually are trained therapists. Others have been 'ball busting', high flyers in the world of business, commerce or teaching. Many will apprentice themselves initially to other, more experienced, mistresses at the outset of their careers in order to learn their dungeon craft. Almost without exception, these women are well educated, intelligent and highly skilled communicators.

The world of the dominatrix encompasses all facets of human desire and imagination. It is a world where eroticism coexists with horror, humour and downright weirdness; while fantasy merges with madness, you will encounter many outrageously funny incidents in the life of the dominatrix, from the submissive who wanted his artificial leg put into bondage to the 'kinky' kidnap that went hilariously wrong, plus a whole lot more besides...

www.magnolia-books.com

www.ingramcontent.com/pod-product-compliance
Lightning Source LLC
Chambersburg PA
CBHW020532290526
45786CB00002B/845